Energy Policy

Edited by Tolga Taner

Published in London, United Kingdom

IntechOpen

Supporting open minds since 2005

Energy Policy
http://dx.doi.org/10.5772/intechopen.77437
Edited by Tolga Taner

Contributors
Akihiro Otsuka, Collins Ayoo, Matjaz Prek, Himanshu Dehra, Tatsujiro Suzuki, Faisal Al Musa, Tolga Taner

First published in London, United Kingdom, 2020 by IntechOpen
IntechOpen is the global imprint of INTECHOPEN LIMITED, registered in England and Wales, registration number: 11086078, 7th floor, 10 Lower Thames Street, London, EC3R 6AF, United Kingdom
Printed in Croatia

British Library Cataloguing-in-Publication Data
A catalogue record for this book is available from the British Library

Additional hard and PDF copies can be obtained from orders@intechopen.com

Energy Policy
Edited by Tolga Taner
p. cm.
Print ISBN 978-1-78923-873-0
Online ISBN 978-1-78923-874-7
eBook (PDF) ISBN 978-1-83962-954-9

For EU product safety concerns:
IN TECH d.o.o., Prolaz Marije Krucifikse Kozulić 3, 51000 Rijeka, Croatia, info@intechopen.com or visit our website at intechopen.com.

Meet the editor

Associate Professor Dr. Tolga Taner, PhD, has been the Head of the Department of Motor Vehicles and Transportation Technology at the Aksaray University since 2012. He received his BSc degree in Mechanical Engineering in 1998, his MSc degree in Mechanical Engineering from Pamukkale University, Denizli, Turkey, in 2002, and his PhD degree in Mechanical Engineering from the Gazi University of Engineering Faculty, Ankara, Turkey, in 2013. In 2018, Inter-University Council (UAK) gave Dr. Taner the title of associate professor. He also worked as a lecturer (part-time) in the Department of Technical Programs, Middle East Technical, from 2003 to 2006. His current research interests include exergy, renewable energy, and proton exchange membrane fuel cells. He has published many scientific and conference papers and books. In addition, he has been a manager and researcher in many research projects.

Contents

Preface

This book, which concerns a general and specific technical level of energy politics, deals with the policy effects of energy supply and exploits its economic, social, planning, and environmental aspects.

This book will encourage both academic research and national energy policy. From concept to publication, this book took approximately two years to complete.

I thank the publisher, IntechOpen, in particular the Author Service Manager Ms. Romina Skomersic, for her support, help, and guidance. I also thank all the chapter authors for their sterling efforts. Finally, I thank all my family, my wife Öznur, and my daughter Özüm for their support.

I hope that this book will be helpful to those interested in energy politics. Therefore, this book will make a scientific contribution to energy policy for governments, researchers, academics, graduate (BSc and MSc) and doctoral (PhD) students, and other scientists both today and in the future.

Dr. Tolga Taner, PhD
Associate Professor,
Head of the Department of Motor Vehicles and Transportation Technologies,
Aksaray University,
Aksaray, Turkey

Section 1

Introduction to the Energy

Chapter 1

Introductory Chapter: Trends and General Information on Energy Policies in the World

Tolga Taner

1. Introduction

This book is a comprehensive book of energy policies. It includes the technical meaning of energy as well as energy policies. In addition to the global scope of energy, it also explains what needs to be done in countries. In the studies, the works made in terms of energy from countries are also presented. Solutions for the energy problem that will continue to form the world of the future are also emphasized. It is obvious that the improvements to be made in energy can minimize the problems between countries in the future.

2. General evaluation of energy policies

Energy needs to be well described before referring to energy policies. Energy includes many phenomena as well as the ability to move. Force creates heat and its derivatives, as it forms the basis of energy. The basic phenomena that make up energy are the kinetic and potential energies as well as the internal energy of the system and/or matter. Energy is a fundamental concept that plays a role in the creation of the universe and planets. In fact, energy such as water energy is a needed resource and is a resource that humanity will always need.

Energy has been utilized in pre-ages, middle ages, and recent times. Humanity has faced many problems and wars in order to secure energy sources. These situations have continued for ages and still continue today. Primary energy resources are the leading ones, and the most important of these are oil, natural gas, and similar energy sources.

In this chapter, it is suggested to solve the energy crisis and problems in a neutral way. Before that, some studies should be mentioned in the literature.

Energy efficiency optimization processes need to be analyzed not only for countries but also for industries as well as for energy consumption [1].

Applications of thermodynamics and heat transfer principles from engineering knowledge are also essential for energy saving in industry processes, in finding energy and exergy efficiencies. Economic analysis should be applied for improvements in energy policy, energy and exergy efficiency results, and energy and exergy efficiency improvements based on existing and regulated scenarios [2].

Alternative energy options have become a serious source of energy due to depletion of fossil fuels. These energy resource options bring about important experimental and prototype studies in order to realize alternative energy and renewable energy systems [3].

It is also necessary to mention the energy economy of renewable energy sources. There are many different studies in the literature on energy economy. In addition to the economic analysis of a wind power plant, there have been some previous studies on the feasibility of wind power plants [4, 5]. The literature includes proton exchange membrane (PEM) fuel cell from other energy systems [6–8]. There is a study on solar energy, which is another renewable energy source, and there is a feasibility study that also includes techno-economic analysis of solar energy [9].

In addition, the implementation of the energy management program plays a meaningful role in achieving the target of energy policies to ensure efficiency in management of renewable energy sources [10]. When determining energy policies, countries should implement the energy management program in industries as a solution. In this way, countries save energy by controlling energy more efficiently and faster.

3. Overview of world energy and aspect of energy policy

Energy policies are now being developed on a long-term basis in developed and developing countries. Globally, the supply of energy to the world is becoming more challenging as the population increases. Countries develop many strategies and plans considering energy while developing strategies. Many countries are turning to alternative and renewable energy sources due to the exhaustion of primary energy sources as well as the emission of pollutants in the environment.

Regarding the power sector, renewable energy systems are growing in the energy sector. As of 2018, 188 GW were installed globally. However, the new power capacity increases have finally stabilized after years of growth. Global renewable energy systems have increased their power capacity to approximately 2378 GW, combining fuel and nuclear power systems. In 2018, more than 90 countries had installed at least 1 GW. Approximately 30 countries have exceeded 10-GW production capacity. Interest in wind and solar PV systems continues to grow and its share in mixed renewable energy systems is growing by approximately 20% in countries [11].

In the transportation sector, the use of renewable energy systems at a lower level is a handicap. Biofuels are popular among renewable energy sources and systems as well as the energy market for home and industry. In particular, interest in electric vehicles with no air pollutants has been increasing worldwide. In addition to the 63% increase in the number of global electric cars, electric bus fleets are gaining importance in cities [11].

In heating and cooling, procurement of energy systems related to renewable energy sources is slow due to energy policy problems. Due to integrated policy approaches, it increases the demands and purchases of energy efficiency in renewable energy sources with the help of advanced technologies [11].

Technological advances in renewable energy sources have seen that the power sector has grown further than the heating, cooling, and transport sector. The main reason for this is that the costs involved in conventional thermal production have become more advantageous compared to renewable energy sources and consequently the tendency toward the power sector increases.

In **Table 1**, indicators of renewable energy can be seen clearly. Renewable energy investment cost was 326 [$ billion] in 2017. In 2018, investment in renewable energy fell to 289 [$ billion] annually. The capacity of renewable power with hydropower existed 2,197 [GW] for 2017 year and 2,378 [GW] for 2018 year. The capacity of renewable power without hydropower became from 1,081 to 1,246 [GW] for a one year. The capacity of hydropower was 1,132 [GW], the capacity of wind power was 591 [GW], the capacity of solar energy with photovoltaic happened 505 [GW], the capacity of bioenergy power was 130 [GW] the capacity of geothermal power got

Investment of the renewable energy	**Cost of investment**	**Year 2017**	**Year 2018**
Annual renewable energy investment related to power	[$ billion]	326	289
Power obtained from the renewable energy	**Unit of power**	**Year 2017**	**Year 2018**
Capacity of obtaining renewable power with hydropower	[GW]	2197	2378
Capacity of obtaining renewable power without hydropower	[GW]	1081	1246
Capacity of hydropower	[GW]	1112	1132
Capacity of wind power	[GW]	540	591
Capacity of obtaining solar energy with photovoltaic devices	[GW]	405	505
Capacity of bioenergy power	[GW]	121	130
Capacity of geothermal power	[GW]	12.8	13.3
Capacity of concentrating solar thermal power	[GW]	4.9	5.5
Capacity of ocean power	[GW]	0.5	0.5
Capacity of bioelectricity generation annually	[TWh]	532	581
Heat of the renewable energy	**Unit of power**	**Year 2017**	**Year 2018**
Capacity of solar hot water	[GWth]	472	480
Transport of the renewable energy	**Unit of power**	**Year 2017**	**Year 2018**
Production of ethanol annually	Liters (billion)	104	112
Production of biodiesel (fatty acid methyl esters) annually		33	34
Production of biodiesel (hydrotreated vegetable oil) annually		6.2	7.0

Table 1.
Indicators of renewable energy in the world [11].

13.3 [GW], the capacity of concentrating solar thermal power became 5.5 [GW] and the capacity of ocean power was 0.5 [GW] in 2018. The capacity of bioelectricity generation for annual became 581 [TWh]. In addition, when comparing biodiesel production capacity from renewable energies with others, it is seen that biodiesel production is at sufficient levels [11].

Figure 1 presents the renewable energy rate for 2018 [11]. These rates are given respectively for: hydroelectric renewable energy capacity, non-hydroelectric renewable energy capacity, wind energy capacity, photovoltaic and solar energy capacity, bioenergy capacity, geothermal energy capacity, solar energy capacity, ocean energy capacity, bioelectric energy capacity as can be seen from the figure. Hydroelectric energy has the highest renewable energy share in the world and its energy share in 2018 is 40%.

In **Table 2**, the energy policy objectives of the countries are carefully questioned [11]. In general, the target numbers of countries' renewable energy sources are presented in the table.

According to **Table 2**, the number of targets for countries with renewable energy targets (national/state/province) reached 169 in 2018. In countries with 100% renewable energy (primary or final energy targets), heating and cooling and transportation targets, the number of targets remains only 1 target. In addition, countries with 100% renewable electricity energy targets reached 65 targets in 2018 [11].

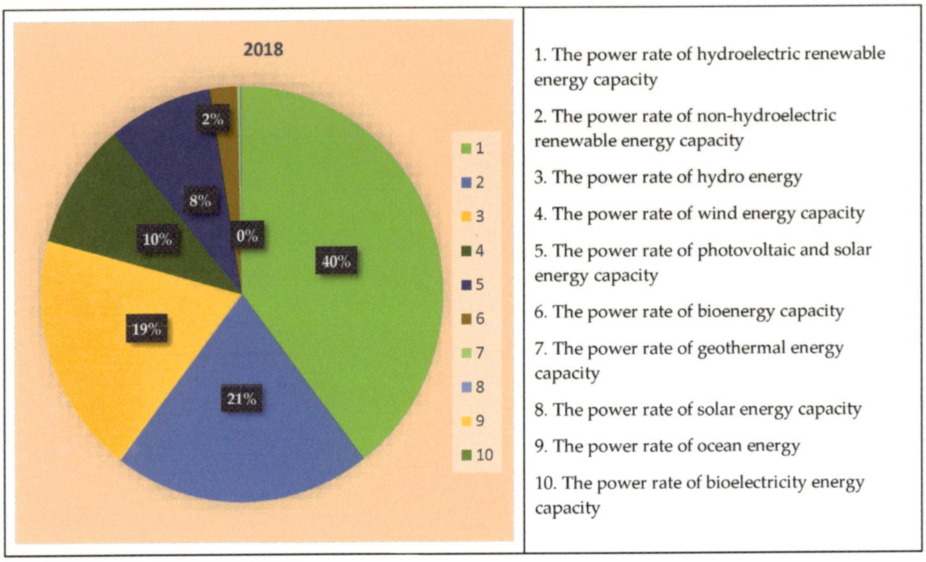

Figure 1.
The power rate of renewable energy in 2018 [11].

Countries with thermal debt and duty (national/state/province based) happened 18 targets in 2018. Countries with biofuel duty (national/state/province based) have been 18 targets in 2018. In briefly, countries with feeding policies (national/state/province based), whose targets became 111, was the highest target in the energy policy [11].

Figure 2 shows the rate of energy policies regarding renewable energy sources for the world in 2018 [11]. These issues can be explained as follows:

Energy policies	Year 2017 (Number of targets)	Year 2018 (Number of targets)
Countries with renewable energy targets (national/state/province based)	179	169
Countries with 100% renewable energy (primary or final energy targets)	1	1
Countries with 100% renewable heating and cooling targets	1	1
Countries with 100% renewable transport targets	1	1
Countries with 100% renewable electricity target	57	65
Countries with thermal debt and duty (national/state/province based)	19	18
Countries with biofuel duty (national/state/province based)	70	70
Countries with feeding policies (national/state/province based)	112	111
Countries with quota policies (national/state/province based)	33	33
Countries participating in the tender held in 2018	29	48
Cumulative tender countries	84	98

Table 2.
Energy policies of renewable energy in the world [11].

Countries with renewable energy targets, Countries with 100% renewable energy, Countries with 100% renewable heating and cooling targets, Countries with 100% renewable transport targets, Countries with 100% renewable electricity target, Countries with thermal debt and duty, Countries with biofuel duty, Countries with feeding policies, Countries with quota policies, Countries participating in the tender held and Cumulative tender countries. When renewable energy resource policies are evaluated, the highest share in renewable energy policies was in the year 2018 with a rate of 29% in the world.

This study shows how the density trend of the final energy is for the world energy policy. Energy density can be explained as the amount of energy per activity of the unit energy output. Thus, it can be seen that if less energy is consumed, the energy density can also be reduced. It is for this reason that the improvement in energy intensity in the world may be brought about by changing some energy policies. Accordingly, the distribution of energy density should be given by years.

Figure 3 indicates an intensity improvement of final global energy. According to the final energy intensity improvement, the ratio between 2000 and 2009 was approximately 1.8%. The change between 2010 and 2014 increased slightly and reached around 2%. In 2015, the energy intensity improvement ratio increased further and exceeded 2%. As of 2016, the trend was downward and approached around 1.5% in 2018 [12].

Figure 4 shows the intensity increase of the final country/region energy. According to the highest of the final energy intensity improvement, the ratio between 2000 and 2009 was occurred approximately 3.0% in the India. The change between 2010 and 2014 was happened around 3.8% in the China. In 2015, the energy intensity improvement ratio increased further and exceeded 5% in the India. China's energy intensity approached around 5.8% in 2016, 5.6% in 2017 and approximately 5.0% in 2018, respectively [12].

Figure 5 shows the global primary energy intensity improvement rate. In case of technical efficiency in global energy intensity improvement rate, changes in energy intensity improvement rate are observed in **Figure 5**. Technical efficiency remains

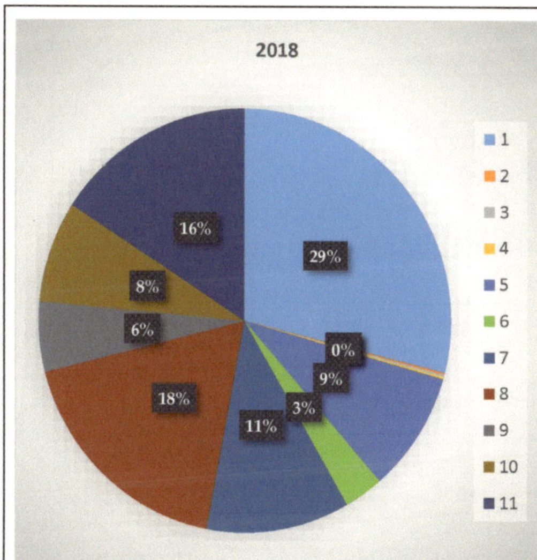

1. Countries with renewable energy targets
2. Countries with 100% renewable energy
3. Countries with 100% renewable heating and cooling targets
4. Countries with 100% renewable transport targets
5. Countries with 100% renewable electricity target
6. Countries with thermal debt and duty
7. Countries with biofuel duty
8. Countries with feeding policies
9. Countries with quota policies
10. Countries participating in the tender held
11. Cumulative tender countries

Figure 2.
Rate of the energy policies of renewable energy for the world in 2018 [11].

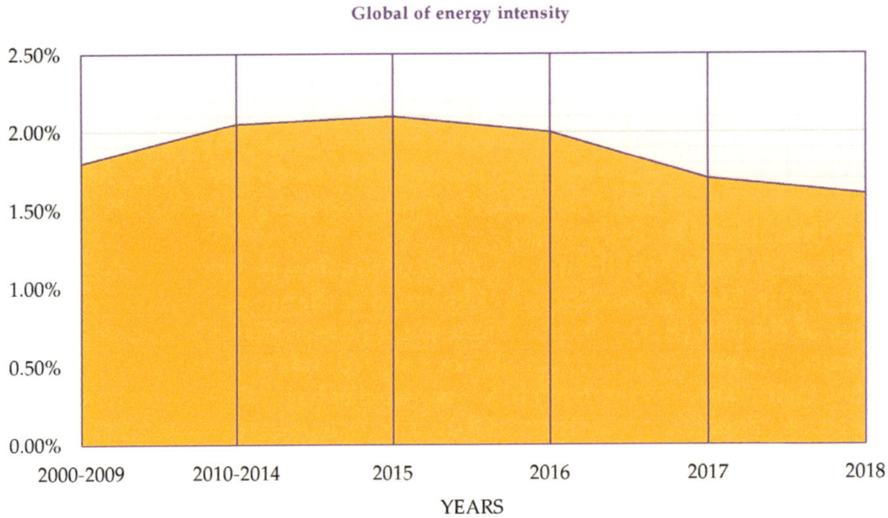

Figure 3.
Global intensity improvement of final energy [12].

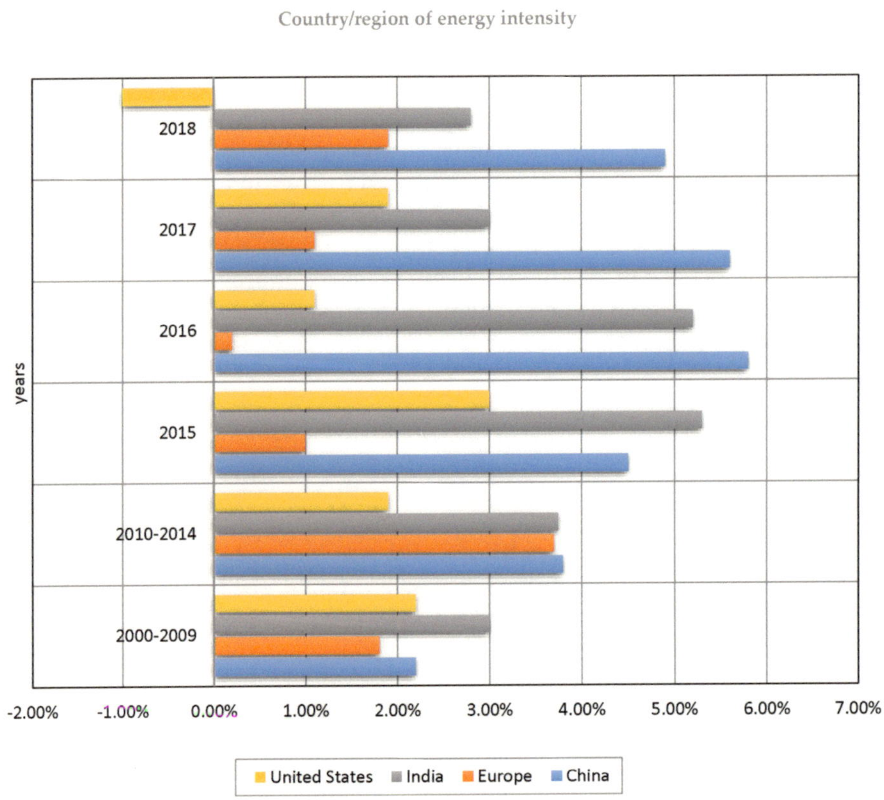

Figure 4.
Country/region's intensity improvement of final energy [12].

the main driver of energy density improvements. Global technical efficiency improvements between 2015 and 2018 prevented 4% more energy consumption in 2018. This technical efficiency has doubled the global primary energy intensity improvement rate in 2018 [12].

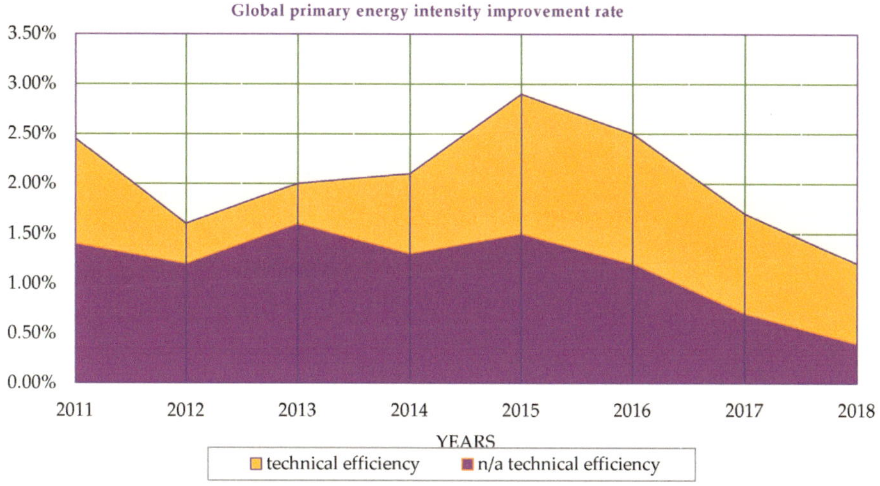

Figure 5.
Global primary energy intensity improvement rate [12].

This book discusses the current world situation regarding the existing energy policies. The interest in energy sources and energy data for renewable energy sources are presented and the energy distribution shares are clearly shown in detail. The biggest problem in energy policies is still the investment cost. Currently, materials and systems of energy systems occupy a significant place in energy conversion. Energy costs can be improved with advanced technological systems.

4. Results and discussion

In this section, it is necessary to determine the global energy targets as well as the current energy data. Energy policies should be considered in the short-term as well as long- and medium-term plans. In short, countries have to take all kinds of measures in their energy policies and wars, turmoil, government stabilization, and human rights into consideration.

Accordingly, in order to shape the world of, the future, 2050 and beyond, arrangements should be made by taking into account the data that can shed light on energy policies.

The increase in geopolitical tensions as well as many other uncertainties such as the oil crises in the world affect the energy policies [13]. In addition, precautions must be taken urgently for emissions-particles and other key factors released during energy production. While energy policies affect these phenomena mentioned above, energy investment costs and system installations are other factors. In addition, disagreements, unrest and wars between countries directly affect energy policies.

Due to key factors, when it is evaluated in terms of countries, it is necessary to reveal what should be done in energy policies in the coming years. Laws and objectives should be regulated accordingly [13]. Governments should focus on sustainable energy resources and sound steps should be taken forward. Stability and order can only be achieved through the establishment and implementation of good energy policies.

The energy history chronology and future energy scenario are presented in **Figure 6**. In 1919, energy consumption was only 1500 Mtoe, while in 2018 it was 14,300 Mtoe. In 1919, only wood, coal, and small amounts of oil were consumed,

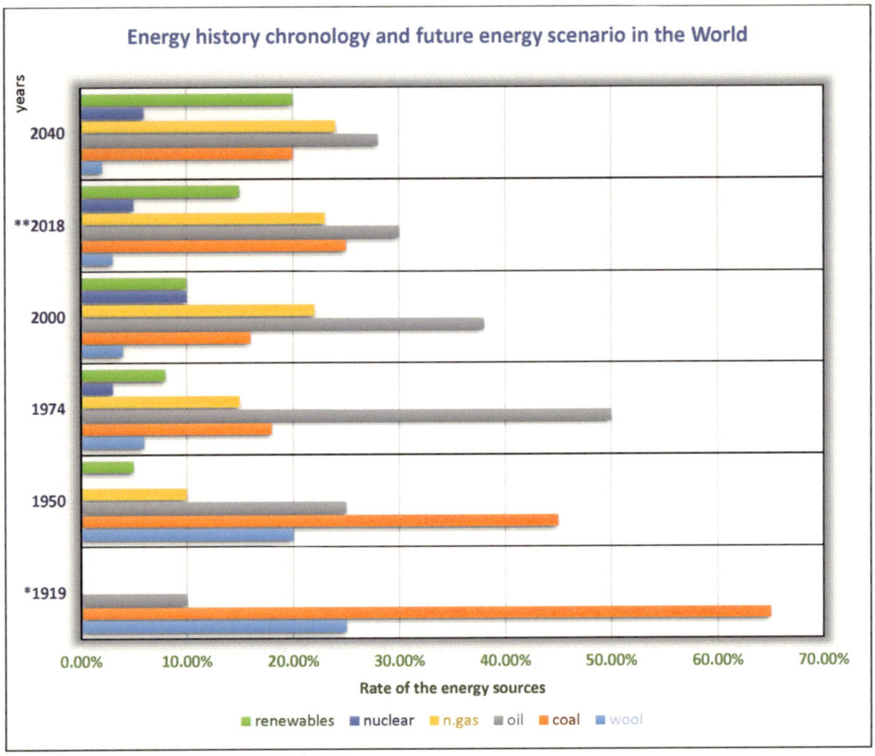

*Notes: * 1,500 [Mtoe] & ** 14,300 [Mtoe]*

Figure 6.
*Energy history chronology and future energy scenario in the world [13]. Notes: * 1,500 [Mtoe] & ** 14,300 [Mtoe].*

but in 2018 this changed completely. In 2018, petroleum was the first, followed by natural gas. Immediately after, coal and natural gas consumption are listed. Interest in renewable energy sources has also increased. In the 2040 forecasts, petroleum and natural gas are in the forefront, while coal and renewable energy sources are visually equalized in terms of consumption. It is foreseen that the consumption in nuclear energy may be considerable [13].

5. Conclusion

This book indicates the policy of energy in the world. Energy wars continue to occur due to the energy policies of the countries in the world. Energy policies in recent years have a direct impact on the development of countries. Countries are taking steps towards existence by producing short, medium and long term energy strategies. It is also explained in the concluding section on how energy in the general context might be in the future.

There are many factors in the decisions and measures taken regarding energy policies. It is clear that it will play a key role in global warming, as well as the factors that will affect countries' investment costs, geopolitical locations, emissions, and other energy policies.

In **Figure 7**, the energy efficiency now and future energy scenario in the world are emphasized [14]. There has been a decline in the energy consumption curve starting from 2010. According to the forecasts of 2050, energy density ratio is expected to increase while per capita energy consumption decreases. By 2050,

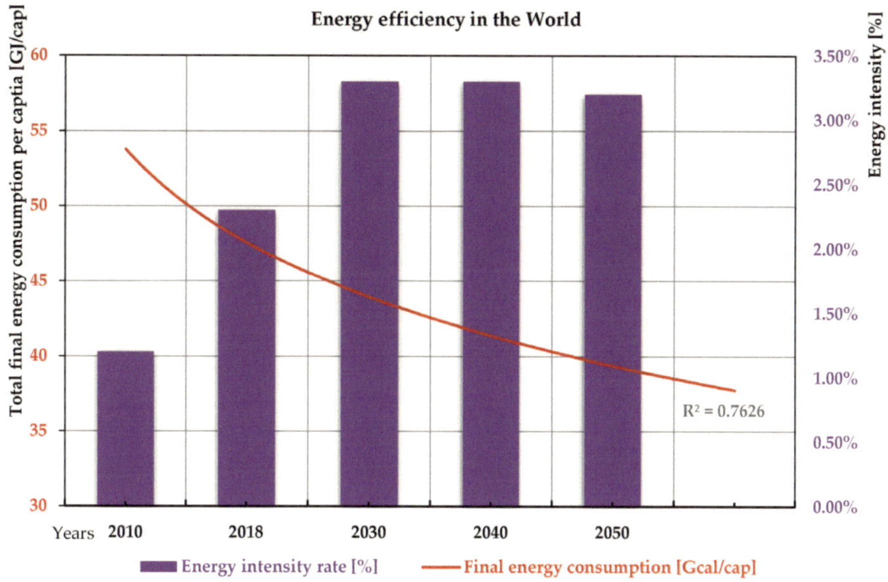

Figure 7.
Energy efficiency now and future energy scenario in the world [14].

energy density and energy consumption are expected to become stable. The regression curve shows that the probability is high.

As a result, the energy policies of the countries in the world are causing many problems today. In addition to many global stresses and tensions, the extent of global warming also raises concerns. Energy strategies should be developed by taking into account both energy efficiency and global warming, cross-country crises, population planning, energy investments and systems, legal regulations on energy costs, and many other parameters. Although advances in technologies bring many benefits, the future energy crises should be minimized.

Acknowledgements

I express my gratitude to Intechopen, who sent an invitation for the Fourth Book Editor and Chapter Author. I would like to thank Intechopen's interest and support, and I sincerely hope that similar studies will continue in the future due to Intechopen.

Nomenclature and units

%	energy intensity rate
Energy consumption	Mtoe
GJ/ca	total final energy consumption per captia
GW	gigawatt
Mtoe	million toe
PEM	proton exchange membrane
toe	tonnes of oil equivalent
TWh	terawatt hours

Author details

Tolga Taner
Department of Motor Vehicles and Transportation Technology, Aksaray University, Aksaray, Turkey

*Address all correspondence to: tolgataner@aksaray.edu.tr

References

[1] Taner T. Optimisation processes of energy efficiency for a drying plant: A case of study for Turkey. Applied Thermal Engineering. 2015;**80**:247-260. DOI: 10.1016/j.applthermaleng.2015.01.076

[2] Taner T. Energy-exergy analysis and optimisation of a model sugar factory in Turkey. Energy. 2015;**93**:641-654. DOI: 10.1016/j.energy.2015.09.007

[3] Taner T. Energy and exergy analyze of PEM fuel cell: A case study of modelling and simulations. Energy. 2018;**143**:284-294. DOI: 10.1016/j.energy.2017.10.102

[4] Taner T. Economic analysis of a wind power plant: A case study for the Cappadocia region. Journal of Mechanical Science and Technology. 2018;**32**(3):1379-1389. DOI: 10.1007/s12206-018-0241-6

[5] Taner T, Demirci OK. Energy and economic analysis of the wind turbine plant's draft for the Aksaray city. Applied Ecology and Environmental Sciences. 2014;**2**(3):82-85. DOI: 10.12691/aees-2-3-2

[6] Taner T. Alternative energy of the future: A technical note of PEM fuel cell water. Journal of Fundamentals of Renewable Energy and Applications. 2015;**5**(3):1-4/1000163. DOI: 10.4172/20904541.1000163

[7] Taner T. The micro-scale modeling by experimental study in PEM fuel cell. Journal of Thermal Engineering. 2017;**3**(6):1515-1526. DOI: 10.18186/journal-of-thermal-engineering.331755

[8] Taner T. A flow channel with Nafion membrane material design of Pem fuel cell. Journal of Thermal Engineering. 2018;**5**(5):456-468. DOI: 10.18186/thermal.624085

[9] Taner T, Dalkilic AS. A feasibility study of solar energy-techno economic analysis from Aksaray city, Turkey. Journal of Thermal Engineering. 2019;**3**(5):1-1. DOI: 10.18186/thermal.505498

[10] Taner T, Sivrioglu M, Topal H, Dalkilic AS, Wongwises S. A model of energy management analysis, case study of a sugar factory in Turkey. Sadhana. 2018;**43**(42):1-20. DOI: 10.1007/s12046-018-0793-2

[11] REN21 Secretariat. Renewables 2019 Global Status Report, 1-335. Paris, France: REN21 Secretariat; 2019. ISBN: 978-3-9818911-7-1

[12] International Energy Agency. Energy Efficiency 2019, Energy Efficiency Market Report 2019. 2019. pp. 1-107

[13] International Energy Agency. World Energy Outlook 2019. Paris, France: International Energy Agency; 2019. pp. 1-18

[14] IRENA, International Renewable Energy Agency. Global Energy Transformation: A Roadmap to 2050. 2019 ed. Abu Dhabi: IRENA; 2019. ISBN: 978-92-9260-121-8

Chapter 2

Towards Energy Security for the Twenty-First Century

Collins Ayoo

Abstract

Energy security is a goal that many countries are pursuing to ensure that their economies function without interruption and that their people have access to adequate, reliable and affordable supplies of modern and clean energy. It is a pressing concern because the demand for energy is growing rapidly due to robust economic expansion, population growth, new uses of energy and income growth, and yet the supplies of energy resources required to power these needs are finite and in most cases non-renewable. Furthermore, the production, transportation and utilization of energy are a major source of greenhouse gases that cause global warming and climate change. This chapter examines the multidimensional nature of energy security, presents some indicators that can be used to assess changes in energy security and outlines a range of policy measures that can be used to improve energy security. These include more investments in energy production and transmission; promotion of energy efficiency in various end-use sectors; modernization of the grid to enable the integration of renewables such as wind, solar and geothermal energy into the energy system; undertaking reforms in energy markets to attract private sector investment in energy production, increase competition, reduce wastage and lower costs to energy users and fostering greater international collaboration on energy issues and regional energy trade.

Keywords: energy security, energy security indicators, energy efficiency, renewable energy, energy demand, energy market reforms

1. Introduction

Energy is a critical resource that all economies require to produce goods and services and to enhance human, social, and economic wellbeing [1–4]. It is needed by various industries as an input into the production of goods and services, for transportation, and by households for heating, cooking, lighting and powering domestic appliances. Empirical studies show that energy consumption is positively correlated with indices of economic growth and wellbeing [3]. This is why the provision of energy to most of the world's population has been identified as a criterion for assessing progress towards sustainable development. Both developed and developing countries, however, face a myriad of energy challenges that include inadequate and unsuitable supplies of energy sources, energy supply uncertainties, high and fluctuating prices of energy, and environmental pollution and degradation as a result of the production, distribution, and use of energy. For countries that rely heavily on energy imports from politically unstable regions, additional risks stem from the threats of disruption to energy supplies and the destabilizing effects of such disruptions to their economies and energy markets [5, 6]. Examples of such disruption include the 1973 and 1979 oil crises, the disruption of world oil supplies during the Persian Gulf wars, and the disruption of natural gas supplies to Ukraine in 2014 due to disagreements with Russia [7]. More recently concerns have emerged from energy supply and storage infrastructure due to natural disasters and terrorism. For countries such as the United States, these challenges are intricately linked to their national security. For poor countries, these challenges have undermined their prospects of economic development and constrained their efforts to alleviate poverty and improve the standards of living of their peoples. They have also had an adverse impact on the balance of payments. Addressing these challenges has therefore increasingly become the centrepiece of the energy policies of many countries where the issue is being framed as one of enhancing energy security. This chapter examines energy security with a focus on its nature and meaning, its multiple dimensions, the indicators currently being used to measure energy security, and some policy measures that can be used to enhance energy security.

2. Meaning of energy security

A clear conceptualization of energy security is essential for an efficient and effective pursuit of this policy goal. The literature on energy security is however characterized by widely differing and sometimes inconsistent definitions of the concept. This is partly because various authors on the subject have tended to focus on different sources of risk and conducted studies that differ in the scope of the impacts of the various risks. The International Energy Agency (IEA) that was formed in the 1970s to coordinate a robust response to disruptions to oil supplies defines energy security as the uninterrupted availability of energy sources at an affordable price. Bohi and Toman [8, 9] define energy insecurity as the loss of welfare that may occur as a result of a change in the price or availability of energy. Cherp and Jewell [10] assert that energy security is an instance of security in general and define energy security as "low vulnerability of vital energy systems". Winzer [11] notes that energy security is commonly defined by incorporating the context. Thus, in the United States, the focus of energy security has traditionally been on the reduction of vulnerability to political extortion following the economic hardships experienced in the aftermath of the oil embargo by the Organization of Petroleum Exporting Countries (OPEC) in the 1970s. This is also the reason why policy makers in the United States strongly support the goals of energy independence and raising the shares of renewable energy. Winzer [11] further notes that in several developing countries, the goal of energy security has been to protect the poor against commodity price volatility. He defines energy security as continuity of energy supplies relative to energy demand. According to Andrews [12] and Jun et al. [13], energy security means assuring adequate, reliable supplies of energy at reasonable prices and in ways that do not jeopardize major national values and objectives. Intharak et al. [14] define energy security as the ability of an economy to guarantee the availability of energy supply in a sustainable and timely manner with the energy price being at a level that will not adversely affect economic performance. Their definition thus embodies three fundamental aspects, namely, physical energy security which is the availability and accessibility of energy supply sources; economic energy security which is the affordability of resource acquisition and energy infrastructure development; and, environmental sustainability which entails using energy resources in ways that meet the needs of the present without compromising the ability of future generations to meet their own needs [15]. According to

Grubb et al. [16] and Kruyt et al. [17], security of supply is a system's ability to provide a flow of energy to meet demand in an economy in a manner and price that does not disrupt the course of the economy. They further point out that non-secure energy systems are characterized by sharp energy price increases, reduction in quality, sudden supply interruptions, and long-term disruptions of supply. Sovacool [18–21], Sovacool and Brown [22], Sovacool and Mukherjee [23], Sovacool et al. [24], Brown and Sovacool [25], and Badea et al. [26] define energy security as equitably providing available, affordable, reliable, efficient, and environmentally benign energy services to end users. Brown et al. [27] opine that energy security has to do with questions of reliable energy supplies, regional concentration of energy resources, and the implications of strategic withholding of energy. They point out specific aspects of energy security such as electricity reliability, natural gas and petroleum security, and the vulnerability of the entire energy supply chain. They also maintain that robust global coordination of responses to energy supply shock is critical to energy security. According to APERC [28], energy security consists of 4A's namely, availability, accessibility, acceptability, and affordability.

Although the definitions of energy security provided above are not exhaustive, they all illustrate the importance of energy security, its multi-dimensional nature, and why many countries regard it as a policy priority. In the short-term, energy security concerns focus on the ability of the energy system to react promptly to sudden changes in the supply–demand balance. In the long-term, energy security concerns have to do with timely investments in energy supply in line with economic developments and environmental needs. At the multilateral and global levels, energy security has continued to receive increasing attention as evidenced by Sustainable Development Goal 7 of the United Nations that requires countries to ensure access to affordable, reliable, sustainable, and modern energy for all.

3. Indicators of energy security

Several indicators have been proposed for assessing the energy security risks that various countries face, how the energy security situations have been changing over time, and how energy security is impacted by the energy policies of these countries. Estimates of these indicators are valuable in developing energy security strategies that take into account countries' energy resource endowments, market conditions, vulnerabilities to energy supply shocks, and technological progress. In what follows I present some energy security indicators, explain their use in assessing energy security, and provide energy security metrics for selected countries.

3.1 Energy reserves

Energy reserves refer to the estimated quantity of energy sources (e.g. coal, gas, or oil) known to exist with reasonable certainty, and which can be recovered with presently available technology at an economically viable cost. A country's energy resources and the extent to which they are developed is an important determinant of energy security. In general, countries with vast energy resources are more energy secure compared to those with meagre energy resources. Over time, however, changes can occur that alter a country's energy resources and thus improve or worsen its energy security. For example, the discovery of vast oil and gas resources in the North Sea had a significant impact on Norway's economy and energy security and made Norway a rich oil-exporting country [29]. This is also the case with countries which have recently discovered new energy reserves. **Table 1** presents

	1980	1990	2000	2010	2017
North America	123.3	125.4	232.1	221.5	226.1
South and Central America	26.9	71.5	97.9	325.2	330.1
CIS	67.0	58.4	120.5	144.5	144.9
Europe	16.6	17.5	20.6	13.4	13.4
Middle East	362.4	659.6	696.7	765.9	807.7
Africa	53.4	58.7	93.0	124.5	126.5
Asia Pacific	33.9	36.3	40.1	48.0	48.0
World	**683.5**	**1027.5**	**1300.9**	**1643.1**	**1696.6**

Table 1.
Proved oil reserves in thousand million barrels 1980–2017 [30].

	1980	1990	2000	2010	2017
North America	9.6	9.2	7.2	10.5	10.8
South and Central America	2.8	5.5	7.3	8.1	8.2
CIS	20.5	34.9	40.3	50.0	59.2
Europe	4.2	5.2	4.7	4.4	3.0
Middle East	24.2	37.2	58.3	78.2	79.1
Africa	5.7	9.0	11.9	14.0	13.8
Asia Pacific	4.5	9.0	11.1	14.9	19.3
World	**71.6**	**109.3**	**140.9**	**180.1**	**193.5**

Table 2.
Proved natural gas reserves in trillions of cubic metres [30].

estimates for the proved oil reserves for various geographic regions for selected years from 1980 to 2017. Estimates for natural gas are presented in **Table 2**.

Table 1 shows that the Middle East has the greatest quantity of proven oil reserves followed by North America. Although these two regions account for more than 50% of the world's total proven oil reserves, this fact alone own does not confer on the regions the greatest energy security. Assessing oil security requires a consideration of additional factors such as oil production and consumption and how these are evolving over time. **Table 1** also shows that over time, with the exception of Europe, several regions of the world have reported an increase in their proven oil reserves thus suggesting an improvement in oil security. The case of the United States is particularly significant given that it has in recent years considerably expanded its production and reduced its dependence on oil imports. This has been possible through the shale revolution and also through changes to regulations to permit the drilling and extraction of oil in previously proscribed areas.

Table 2 shows that the Middle East has the largest proven natural gas reserves followed by the CIS. Like the case of oil, most regions of the world have reported an increase in proven natural gas reserves from 1980 to 2017. The exception is Europe whose proven natural gas reserves have declined. The proven reserves of oil and natural gas are a good indicator of the existence or otherwise of potential that can be developed to improve the energy security.

Table 3 shows the proven reserves of coal and the reserve-to-production ratios (R/P ratios) for the various regions at the end of 2017. R/P ratios estimate the time period remaining for the different regions to exhaust their known coal stocks given the current rates of extraction, assuming no changes in existing stocks,

	End of 2017	R/P ratio
North America	258,709	335
South & Central America	14,016	141
CIS	223,228	397
Europe	100,405	159
Middle East and Africa	14,420	53
Asia Pacific	424,234	79
World	**1,035,012**	**134**

Table 3.
Proved coal reserves in millions of tonnes and reserves to production ratio [30].

technologies, or other policies. At the world level, the existing coal reserves can last for about 134 years. The existing coal stocks can last for periods ranging from 53 years for the Middle East and Africa to about 335 years for North America. Based on these results it can be inferred that in the short to medium term, there will be continued energy security with respect to coal availability and utilization. Although concerted efforts are currently being made to reduce the use of coal as part of measures to mitigate climate change, the use of coal will continue to be significant for certain regions of the world. It however implies that coal will play an increasingly smaller role in energy security in the coming years. This could change if significant progress in the carbon capture and storage technologies results in greater use of coal.

3.2 Energy production and consumption

Being the predominant source of energy in most of the world, the production and consumption of oil can serve as a valuable indicator of energy security.

		1980	1990	2000	2010	2017
North America	Production	670.7	654.5	642.5	638.6	916.8
	Consumption	928.4	923.2	1060.6	1040.5	1056.4
South and Central America	Production	194.7	234.0	345.0	378.5	368.3
	Consumption	170.9	176.2	235.1	299.4	317.0
Europe	Production	143.4	217.9	332.5	196.7	162.6
	Consumption	779.2	729.4	762.5	734.2	708.3
CIS	Production	603.2	570.3	396.4	663.1	699.6
	Consumption	421.5	399.1	169.1	178.6	196.3
Middle East	Production	934.0	837.4	1146.9	1220.0	1481.1
	Consumption	93.7	166.5	239.0	356.9	404.4
Africa	Production	300.5	317.0	371.6	481.5	383.3
	Consumption	69.6	95.6	118.4	164.4	189.3
Asia Pacific	Production	244.8	325.9	381.3	403.0	375.5
	Consumption	515.4	664.2	998.3	1302.1	1598.0
World	Production	**3091.3**	**3157.0**	**3616.2**	**3981.4**	**4387.1**
	Consumption	**2978.7**	**3154.1**	**3583.1**	**4076.0**	**4469.7**

Table 4.
Oil production and consumption in millions of tonnes from 1980 to 2017 [30].

The production and consumption of oil for various regions from 1980 to 2017 is shown in **Table 4** and depicted in **Figures 1–8**. At the global scale, both the production and consumption of oil have been growing over time with the oil production consistently matching the oil consumption. This implies that the world has the potential to be energy secure if robust mechanisms are implemented to facilitate the flow of oil from regions with oil surpluses to those with oil deficits. For North America, Europe and Asia Pacific, the oil consumption has consistently exceeded the oil production while for Africa, the Middle East, the CIS, and Central and South America, the oil production has over time been greater than the oil consumption. The United States has for several decades been the largest consumer of oil in the world and has relied considerably on oil imports to bridge the gap between its production and consumption of oil. This has been a major policy concern in the US

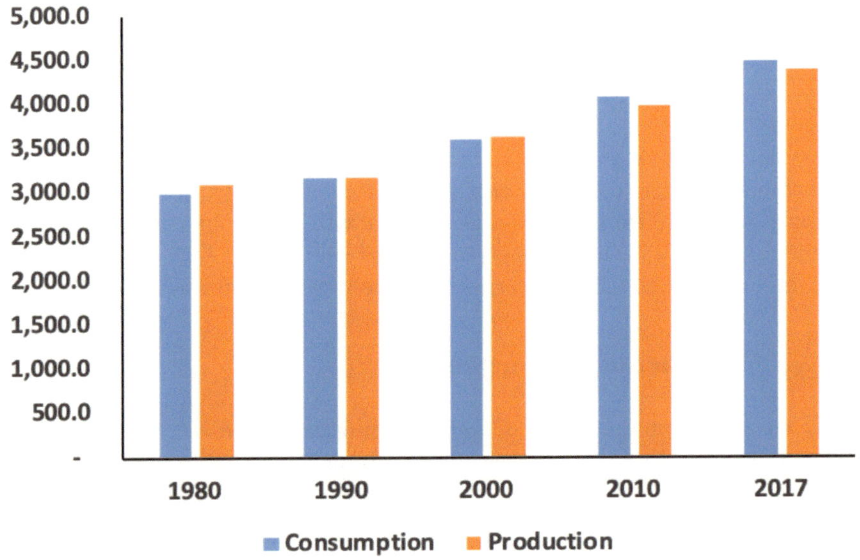

Figure 1.
Oil production and consumption for the world in millions of tonnes from 1980 to 2017 [30].

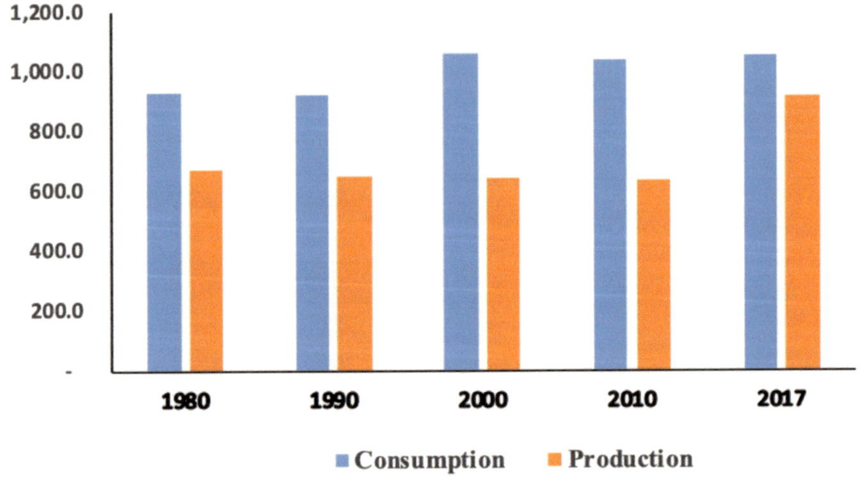

Figure 2.
Oil production and consumption for North America in millions of tonnes from 1980 to 2017 [30].

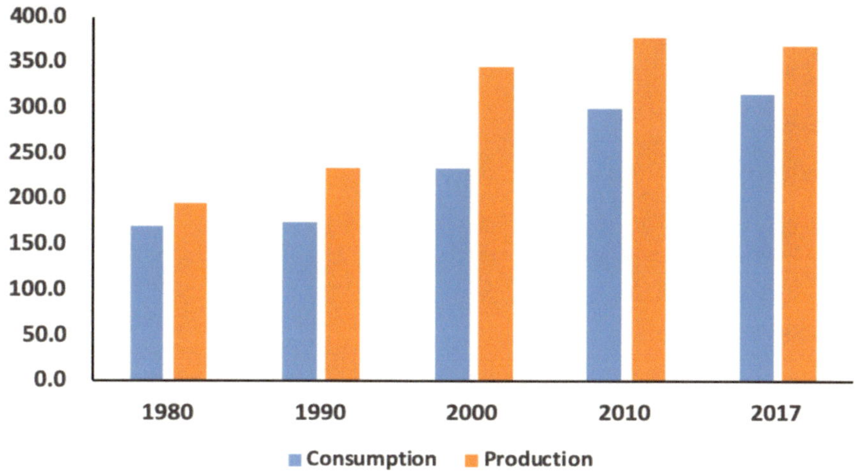

Figure 3.
Oil production and consumption for South and Central America in millions of tonnes from 1980 to 2017 [30].

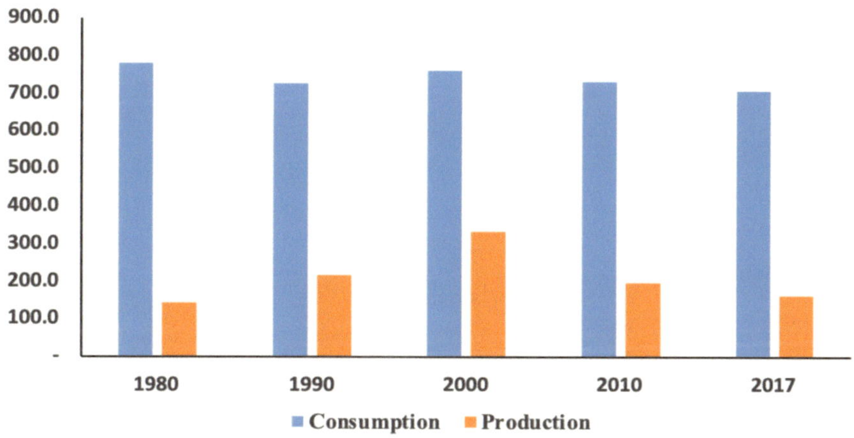

Figure 4.
Oil production and consumption for Europe in millions of tonnes from 1980 to 2017 [30].

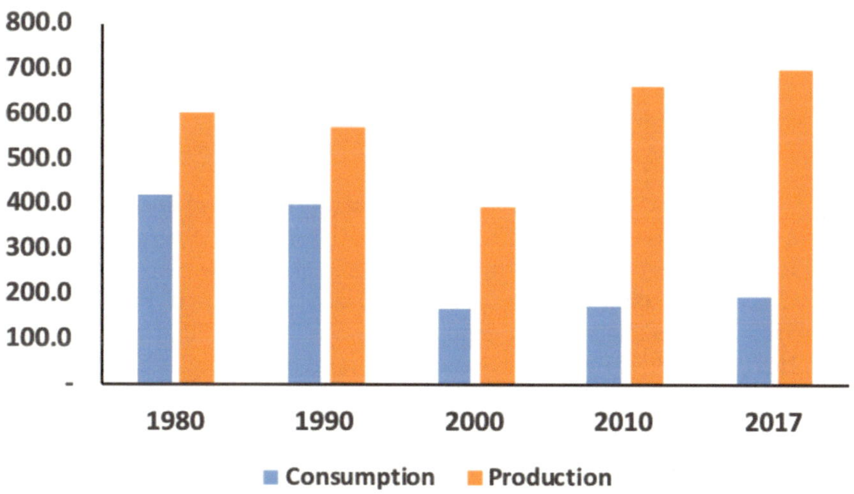

Figure 5.
Oil production and consumption for CIS in millions of tonnes from 1980 to 2017 [30].

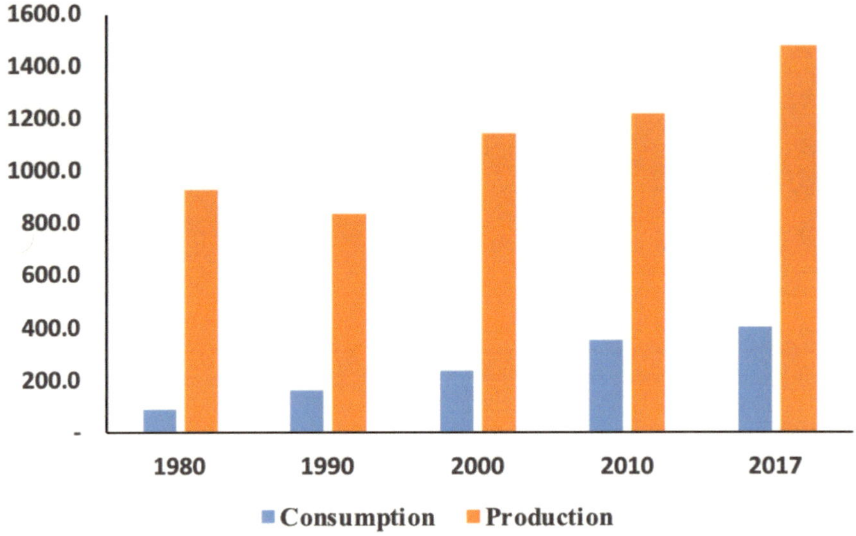

Figure 6.
Oil production and consumption for the Middle East in millions of tonnes from 1980 to 2017 [30].

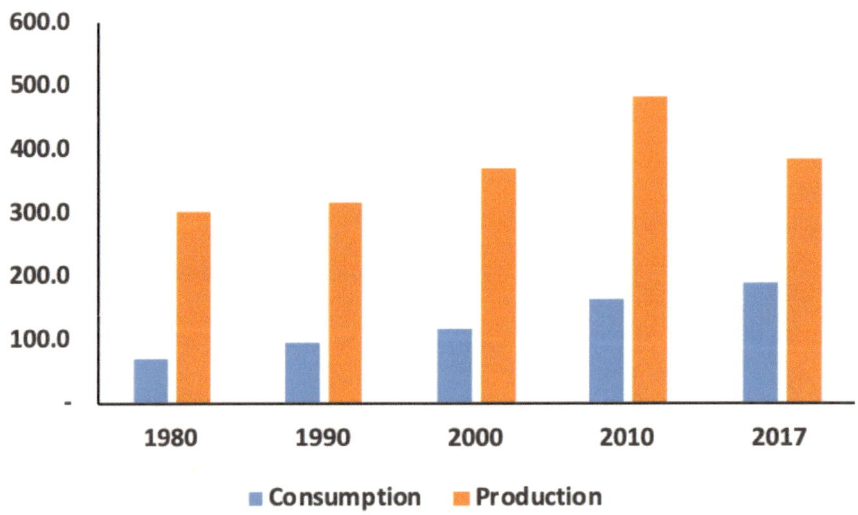

Figure 7.
Oil production and consumption for Africa in millions of tonnes from 1980 to 2017 [30].

and partly explains the country's preoccupation with the goal of energy independence since the oil crises of the 1970s.

The data in **Table 4** also shows that the Middle East and the CIS have had the greatest oil surpluses while Europe has had the greatest oil deficit. From this broad picture that is based on aggregated regional data, we can infer that relative to other regions, Europe and Asia Pacific have the greatest oil insecurity, while the Middle East, Africa, and the CIS are the least oil insecure. In the recent past, the oil consumption in the Asia Pacific has grown rapidly due to its high population and economic growth rates.

Natural gas constitutes a significant share of the energy mix of several countries and contributes critically to their energy security. It is used for heating buildings and water, to cook, to operate refrigeration and cooling equipment, to dry clothes, to provide outdoor lighting, as a fuel in combined heat and power systems, as a fuel to operate compressors that move natural gas through pipelines, to generate electricity, and as a vehicle fuel in the form of compressed natural gas and liquified natural gas. Natural gas is also used as a raw material to produce chemicals, fertilizers and hydrogen.

Table 5 presents data on the production and consumption of natural gas in various world regions from 1970 to 2017. **Figure 9** depicts the global production and consumption of natural gas over the same period. Overall, both the production and

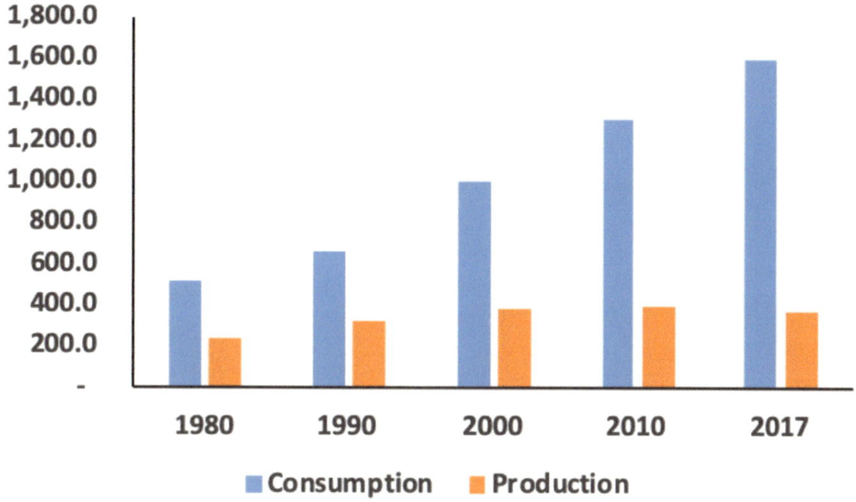

Figure 8.
Oil production and consumption for Asia Pacific in millions of tonnes from 1980 to 2017 [30].

		1970	1980	1990	2000	2010	2017
North America	Production	636.5	621.4	613.2	728.3	775.9	951.5
	Consumption	619.5	605.8	607.6	753.5	803.0	942.8
South & Central America	Production	18.7	35.3	60.3	103.1	163.8	179.0
	Consumption	18.8	36.1	59.6	97.8	150.1	173.4
Europe	Production	104.5	229.5	215.5	293.5	289.5	241.9
	Consumption	108.5	280.7	360.8	484.0	567.7	531.7
CIS	Production	187.5	412.2	764.1	661.6	755.9	815.5
	Consumption	189.5	377.1	632.1	527.2	588.7	574.6
Middle East	Production	10.5	34.4	101.8	206.5	481.6	659.9
	Consumption	9.4	31.9	96.7	185.6	385.6	536.5
Africa	Production	3.0	24.8	72.2	135.1	206.1	225.0
	Consumption	1.6	18.7	39.9	55.7	102.5	141.8
Asia Pacific	Production	15.1	71.9	149.3	277.4	496.5	607.5
	Consumption	14.2	73.6	152.0	298.2	578.3	769.6
World	**Production**	**975.8**	**1429.6**	**1976.3**	**2405.5**	**3169.3**	**3680.4**
	Consumption	**961.4**	**1423.8**	**1948.7**	**2402.0**	**3175.9**	**3670.4**

Table 5.
Natural gas production and consumption in billions of cubic metres from 1970 to 2017 [30].

consumption of natural gas have been increasing over time with the production increasing to match the consumption.

According to the data in **Table 5** and **Figures 10** and **11**, North America, the CIS, the Middle East and Africa produced at least as much natural gas as they consumed in 2017. For the Middle East and the CIS, the natural gas production was significantly higher than the consumption making these regions important global exporters of natural gas. For Europe and Asia Pacific, the production of natural gas has tended to be significantly less than the consumption necessitating the heavy reliance of these regions on large natural gas imports to meet their demands. For the Asia Pacific region, the consumption of natural gas has in recent years been rising rapidly due to robust economic growth and the high population in the region. The

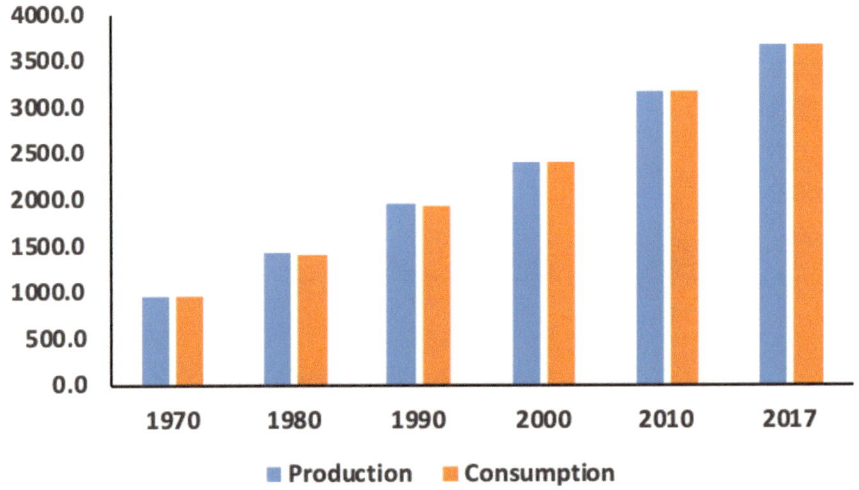

Figure 9.
Global natural gas production and consumption in billions of cubic metres from 1970 to 2017 [30].

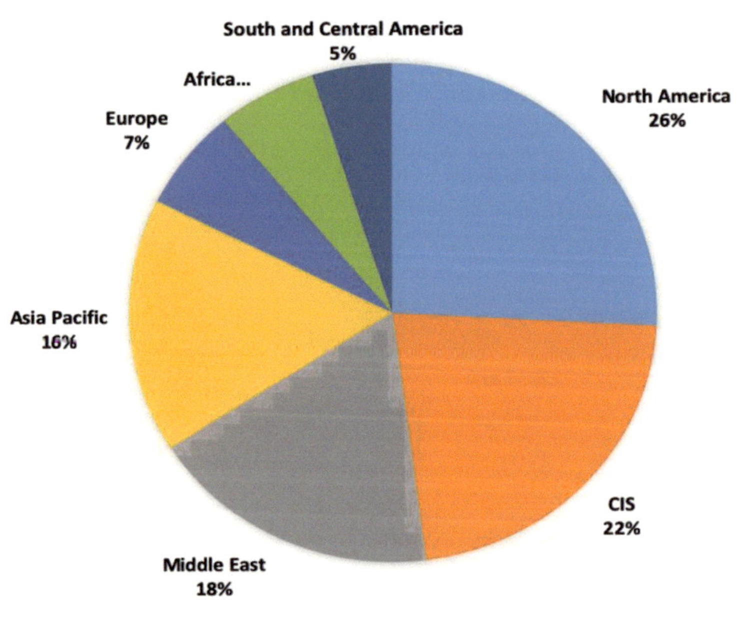

Figure 10.
Regional shares of natural gas production in 2017 [30].

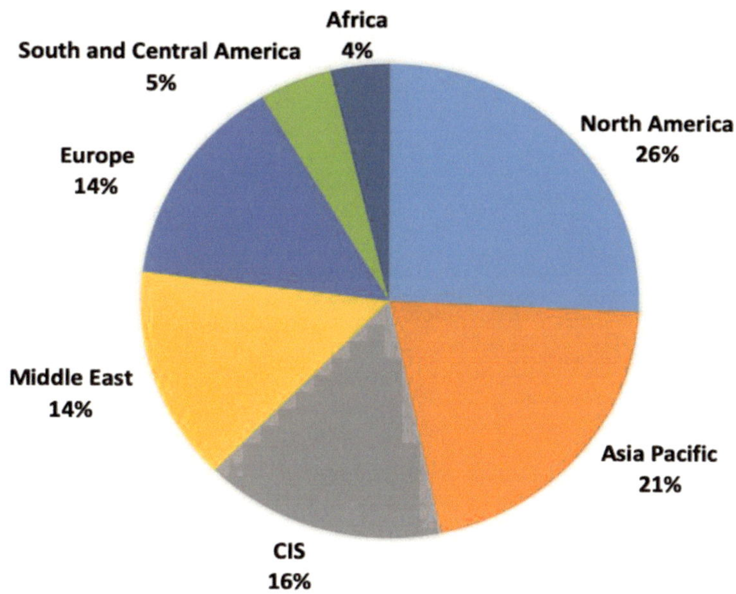

Figure 11.
Regional shares of natural gas consumption in 2017 [30].

situation in Europe is considerably tighter as evidenced by the fact that in 2017 the production of natural gas was less than half the amount consumed in the region thus implying a high dependence on natural gas imports. In the foreseeable future, natural gas security in Europe and the Asia Pacific region will depend on stable, well-integrated efficient natural gas markets that can ensure adequate, reliable and affordable supplies.

The shortage of natural gas in China in the winter of 2017 is a recent example of how the demand and supply of natural gas can impact energy security. The primary cause of the shortage was China's decision to curb reliance on dirty coal so as to reduce urban air pollution and improve the overall quality of the environment. This shift in policy triggered an increase in the demand for natural gas and a rise in its price not only to consumers in China but also for other natural gas importers [31, 32]. The shortage of natural gas in China and the spike in its price occurred despite a glut in global supply and was due to infrastructure and logistical constraints. Achieving natural gas security therefore requires not only initiatives aimed at boosting natural gas production, but also complementary measures such as increased investments in distribution infrastructure and improving LNG shipping capacity.

Electricity is critically important to most economies around the world and its role is expected to increase in the future as countries pursue the goal of decarbonizing their power sectors. Electricity is also important in efforts to eliminate poverty and transform the world into a safe, equitable and environmentally sustainable place [33]. Today, however, many countries are facing massive challenges in electricity security due to rapidly increasing demand and supply constraints. **Table 6** shows the production and consumption of electricity for various regions from 1990 to 2017. With the exception of the CIS where the electricity production fell by about 7% between 1990 and 2017, in all other regions electricity production increased with the greatest percentage increase being in Asia (400%) and the Middle East (387.7%).

The consumption of electricity has been increasing rapidly in most part of the world with the main drivers being industrial and economic growth, and population

		1990	2000	2010	2017	% Change
North America	Production	3701	4658	4982	4963	34.1
	Consumption	3146	4093	4415	4379	39.2
Latin America	Production	605	982	1375	1590	162.8
	Consumption	506	788	1129	1312	159.3
Europe	Production	2900	3438	3865	3886	34.0
	Consumption	2516	2952	3377	3377	34.2
CIS	Production	1676	1250	1483	1566	−6.6
	Consumption	1417	1000	1203	1257	−11.3
Middle East	Production	244	472	892	1190	387.7
	Consumption	213	400	742	977	358.7
Africa	Production	319	446	675	818	156.4
	Consumption	263	379	554	663	152.1
Asia	Production	2259	4024	7983	11,274	399.1
	Consumption	1923	3369	6869	9777	408.4
Pacific	Production	190	253	302	304	60.0
	Consumption	165	218	265	273	65.5

Table 6.
Electricity production and consumption in terawatt Hours (TWH) from 1970 to 2017 [30].

increase. **Figure 12** depicts the consumption of electricity for the various regions in 1990 and 2017. It is evident from **Figure 12** that the greatest absolute increase in electricity consumption over this period occurred in Asia where electricity consumption increased by 408.4% from 1923 TWH to 9777 TWH. Most of the growth in electricity consumption in Asia occurred in China, India, and Japan. Over the 1990–2017 period, the electricity consumption in China increased from 534 TWH to 5683 TWH; that in India increased from 215 TWH to 1156 TWH; and, that in Japan increased from 781 TWH to 1019 TWH. These increases in electricity consumption occurred despite strong energy efficiency improvements.

The electricity production and consumption data for the various regions for 2017 that is plotted in **Figure 13**, shows that although both electricity production and consumption have been increasing over time, the production of electricity exceeded its consumption. Therefore, the inference can be made that at the regional level, potential exists for achieving electricity security in the short to medium term. The broad picture presented in **Figure 13** masks the electricity supply and demand conditions in specific countries and how the electricity is produced and consumed in those countries. It also masks the fact that due to grid and storage losses, not all of the electricity produced is available for consumption.

3.3 Energy trade balances

At particular times, specific countries or regions often have imbalances in their demand and supply of energy that are met through imports and exports. Whether a country is a net importer or exporter of energy is indicated by their energy trade balance that is computed as the difference between energy imports and exports. Countries that are net energy exporters have negative energy trade balances while net energy importers have positive energy trade balances. Based on energy trade

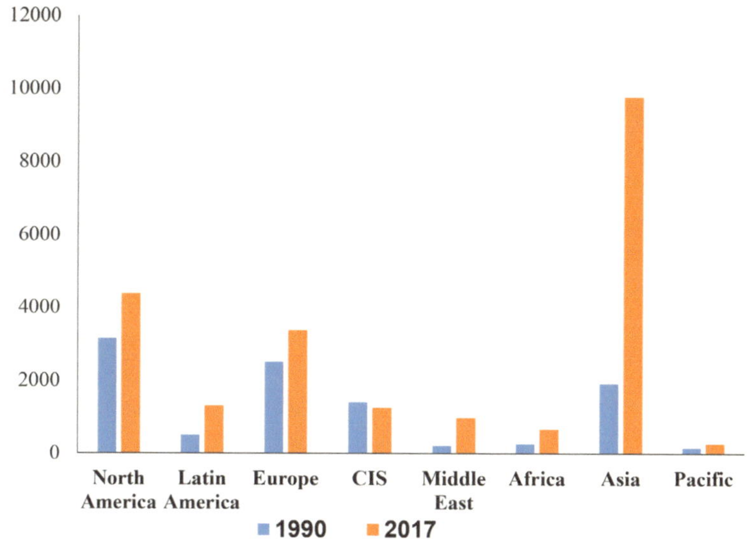

Figure 12.
Electricity consumption in terawatt hours (TWH) for 1990 and 2017 [30].

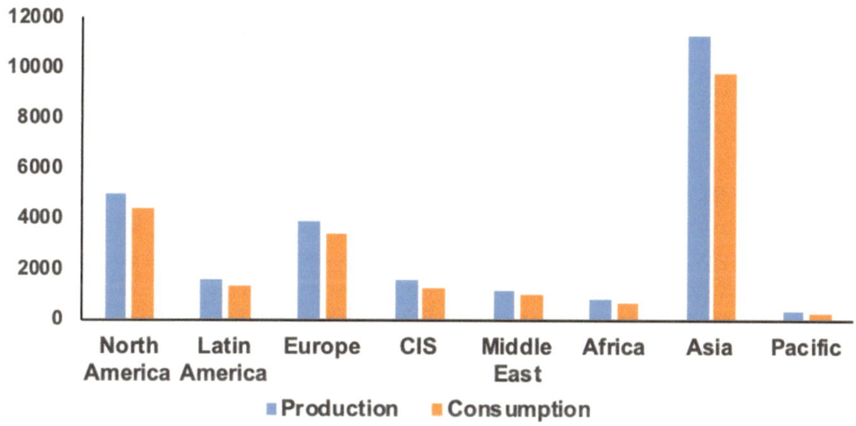

Figure 13.
Electricity production and consumption in terawatt hours (TWH) for 2017 [30].

balances, it can be inferred that regions with positive energy trade balances are more energy insecure compared to those with negative energy trade balances. **Figure 14** depicts the energy trade balances for various regions for 2017 and shows that the largest energy net importers were Asia and Europe and the largest net exporters were the Middle East and the CIS. Europe's energy security situation is precarious because of dwindling energy supplies that have necessitated increasing reliance on energy imports. Importation of less expensive energy into Europe from regions such as the Middle East is a more attractive option compared to more costly efforts to develop the region's own energy resources. As producers of large quantities of cheap energy, the Middle East and the CIS will continue to play a significant role in the global energy scene in the short to medium term. It is worth noting that several major changes are currently occurring in global energy markets and that these changes will have profound implications on energy security in the coming years. An example of such a change is the increase in energy production in the United States that has changed the country's status from a net energy importer to a net energy exporter.

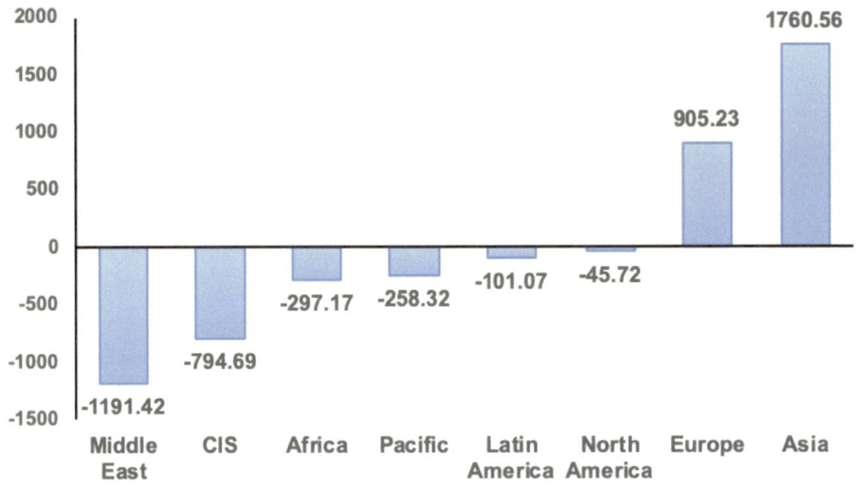

Figure 14.
Energy trade balance in megatons of oil equivalent (Mtoe) in 2017 [30].

3.4 Energy prices

In general, energy prices are determined by the supply and demand conditions in energy markets and also by the policies and regulations such as taxes and subsidies that governments may make to regulate these markets and achieve particular outcomes. Energy prices are an important indicator of energy security to the extent that they embody information about energy scarcity and energy affordability and also play a central role in energy investment decisions. The crude oil prices from 1970 to 2017 are depicted in **Figure 15**. Although the crude oil prices have fluctuated widely over this period, the general trend has been upward. In 1973 the world oil market was significantly impacted by the oil embargo by the Organization of Petroleum Exporting Arab Countries (OPEC) that drastically reduced the supply of oil at a time when the demand for oil was increasing. This action resulted in the price of oil rising from US$ 3 to US$ 12 globally. World oil supplies were again adversely affected in 1979 in the aftermath of the Iranian Revolution and oil prices

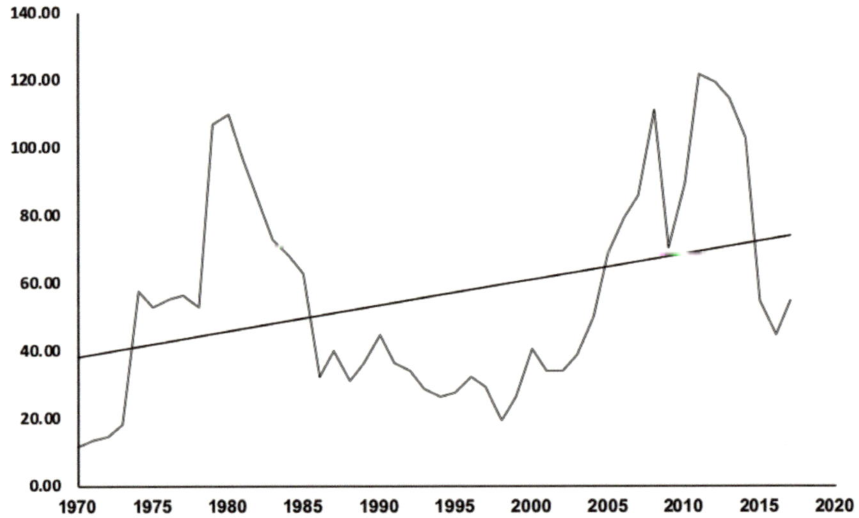

Figure 15.
Crude oil prices from 1970 to 2017 in $ 2017 [30].

increased rapidly from $13 per barrel in mid-1979 to about $34 per barrel in mid-1980. Both these oil shocks threated the energy security of oil-importing countries, reduced economic activity, and increased inflation.

In several developing countries, a significant fraction of the population cannot access modern energy due to the high energy prices. In Kenya, for example, where the majority of the population use Kerosene for cooking and lighting, the price of kerosene has recently risen rapidly thus inducing low income households to reduce their use of kerosene and shift towards wood fuel. Although liquefied natural gas is available, its high price has limited its use to medium and high-income households. Further energy price increases can be expected as energy markets are increasingly deregulated and energy subsidies eliminated. To the extent that these measures reduce energy affordability, they have an adverse effect on household energy security. This brief discussion of energy prices underscores the fact that a strong correlation exists between energy prices and energy security and that, in general, energy security will be compromised when energy prices are rising rapidly. These broad conclusions can be extended to other energy sources such as electricity and natural gas.

3.5 Energy diversity

All else equal, economies that depend on a limited portfolio of non-renewable energy sources are less energy secure compared to those endowed with an abundance of diverse energy supplies [34]. Energy systems that are diverse are more resilient and adaptable to shocks in energy supplies. The Russian-Ukrainian gas crisis is an example of the vulnerability that can result from dependence on a single supplier of energy. In January 2006 following disagreements about the price of natural gas and the cost of transit, Russia cut off all gas supplies passing through Ukraine thus adversely affecting several European nations. In January 2009, disagreements about natural gas price again resulted in the disruption of natural gas supplies from Russia to 18 European nations. The severity of this threat to Europe's energy security stems from the fact that Russia provides about 25% of the natural gas consumed in the European Union and that approximately 80% of natural gas exports from Russia to the European Union are through pipelines across Ukraine. The Southern Gas Corridor (SGC) was started as a response to the overdependence of many countries in Central and South East Europe on Russia to meet most or all of their natural gas requirements. The overarching goal of the SGC was to enhance EU's energy security by diversifying the routes and sources of gas supplies to the EU [35, 36]. This strategic objective has been achieved through the construction of a system of pipelines that can bring natural gas from the Caspian Basin, Central Asia, the Middle East, and the Eastern Mediterranean Basin into Europe thus reducing the dependence on Russian natural gas supplies [35].

The contribution of diversity to energy security also applies to other domains such as transportation fuels and the generation of electricity. In the transportation sector, the fuels that are mostly used are gasoline and diesel due to their high energy content. Some measures that are currently being undertaken to enhance transportation energy security are developing and promoting the use of alternative fuels such as ethanol, natural gas, biodiesel, hydrogen, propane, methanol and electricity (as in the case of battery-powered electric and fuel-cell vehicles). In addition to reducing dependence on fossil fuels, the use of these alternative fuels has been cited as having the potential to drastically lower the emissions of greenhouse gases and thus mitigate the risk climate change. There are however several controversies associated with the increased use of alternative transportation fuels as a strategy for diversifying the energy mix. For example, the simulation model developed by

Chen et al. [37] shows that although promoting greater production of food-based biofuels reduces overall fossil fuel use, it leads to a marginal reduction in the global greenhouse emissions, and a large increase in food prices. Flynn [38] noted that the adoption of compressed natural gas as an alternative transportation fuel in Canada and the United States had been slow and below the critical level which would enable suppliers to survive in a competitive market. The reasons for this outcome include the high cost of hybrid cars relative to conventional cars, the lack of infrastructure to support converted vehicles, lack of refuelling facilities, and the failure of existing refuelling stations to achieve profitability.

Diversifying electric power generation is an area that several countries are increasingly focusing on to enhance their overall energy security. It is driven by the increase in the demand for electricity due to factors such as population growth, greater use of electrical appliances and equipment, and the need reduce emissions of greenhouse gases. In a country such as the United States, the main energy sources for electric power generation are coal, natural gas, nuclear power and hydro. The amounts of electricity produced from these sources are shown in **Figure 16**. Although coal and nuclear power have dominated electricity production, a significant change has occurred leading to reduced use of these fuels for electricity production and greater use of natural gas that is cheaper, cleaner, and more abundant.

3.6 Share of renewable energy

In general, economies that depend on a limited portfolio of non-renewable energy sources are less energy secure than those that are endowed with abundant renewable energy sources. Renewable energy resources are attractive because their supplies are unlimited and inexhaustible so that, unlike non-renewable sources, their consumption today does not reduce the flows available in the future. If adequately developed, they can substitute for non-renewable energy and underpin the transition needed in the energy system to sustainably power economic growth and ameliorate the threat of climate change. Some of the common renewable energy resources that can be harnessed to improve energy security are biomass, hydropower, solar, wind, and geothermal energy. Presently, increasing the share of

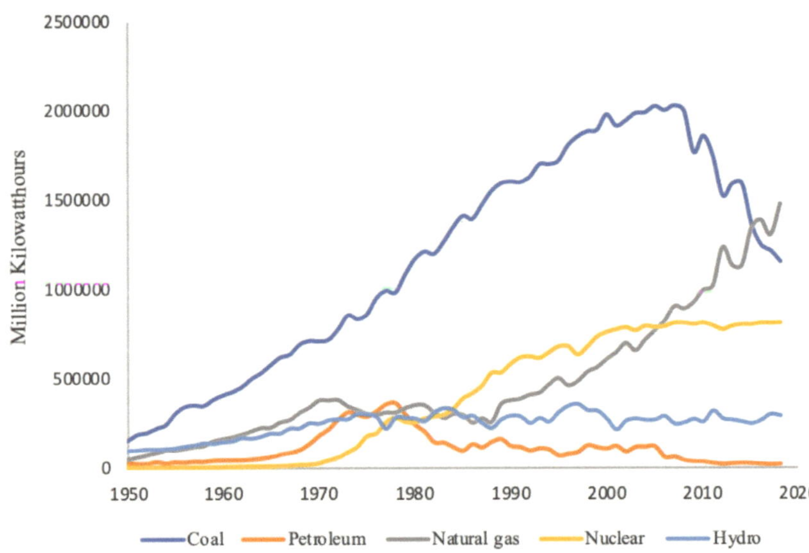

Figure 16.
Electricity generation in US by energy source [30].

renewables in the final energy consumption is a policy priority of many countries as evidenced by the European Union's goal of generating 20% of its electricity from renewables by 2020 [39]. Similarly, the United States has regulations (known as the renewable portfolio standard or renewable electricity standard) obligating electricity supply companies to produce a specific fraction of their electricity from renewable energy sources [40]. In Germany, the Renewable Energy Act mandates that 35% of electricity be produced from renewable sources in 2020 and that this share be increased to 80% by 2050. **Table 7** presents data on the consumption of renewables in the US electric power sector from 1984 to 2018. Over this period, the US electric power sector experienced a significant increase in the use of renewables with wind and solar playing a dominant role. The data in **Table 7**, shows that in 2000, the share of wind and solar in the renewables used to produce electricity was only 2% and that this increased to 49% in 2018. The combined use of wind and solar in electricity production in the US is shown in **Figure 17** and the combined share of wind and solar in the total renewable energy used in the electric power sector is shown in **Figure 18**. The increased use of wind and solar energy has been facilitated by technological innovation and has not only contributed to the diversification of the energy system but also provided several other benefits such improvement in health, savings from reduced fossil use, reduced emissions of greenhouse gases, industrial growth, and the creation of thousands of clean manufacturing jobs.

	Hydro	Geothermal	Solar	Wind	Wood	Waste	Biomass	Total renewable
1984	3352.81	80.81	0.06	0.07	4.82	4.43	9.25	3442.99
1990	3014.01	160.55	3.82	29.01	128.52	187.99	316.51	3523.89
1995	3149.39	137.96	5.12	32.63	125.41	296.25	421.66	3746.77
2000	2767.92	143.76	5.03	57.06	134.32	318.43	452.75	3426.52
2005	2670.13	146.90	5.50	178.09	184.97	220.72	405.70	3406.32
2010	2521.49	148.48	11.76	923.27	195.60	263.78	459.37	4064.37
2015	2307.72	148.34	227.90	1775.71	243.86	281.02	524.88	4984.54
2018	2672.51	153.81	606.97	2530.41	215.11	280.03	495.14	6458.83

Table 7.
Renewable energy use in US electric power sector in trillion of Btu [30].

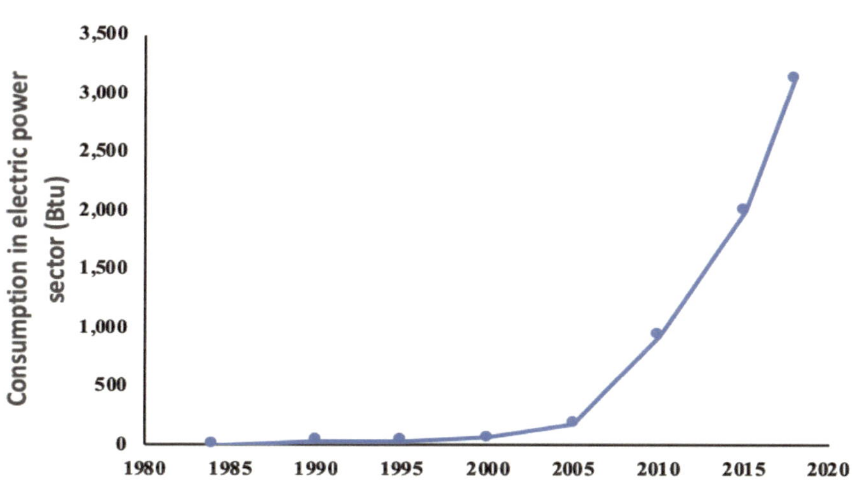

Figure 17.
Combined wind and solar consumption in US electric power sector from 1980 to 2018 (Trillions Btu) [30].

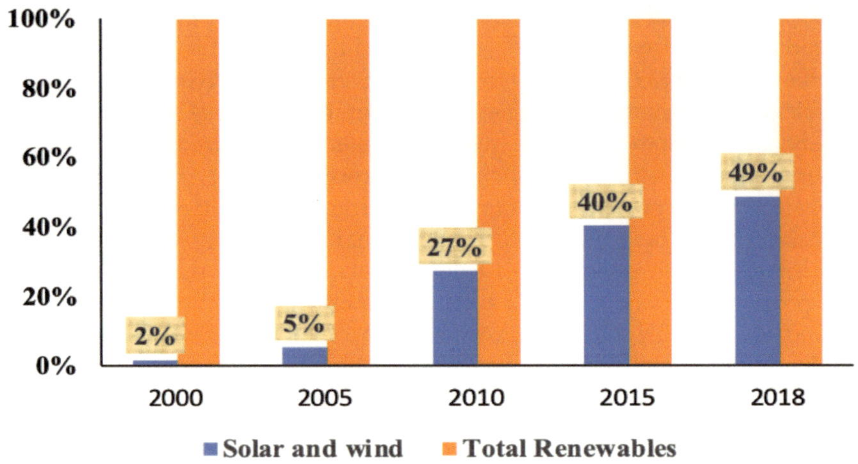

Figure 18.
Share of combined wind and solar in US electric power sector [30].

Further growth in the use of wind and solar power can be expected in the future as the market costs of these technologies continue to fall and as progress is made to overcome the challenges of intermittency.

4. Policy instruments for improving long-term energy security

Energy resources are indispensable to all economies where they are used to power economic growth and to provide households with critical services such as heating, lighting, cooking, and operating equipment and appliances. A secure energy system is vital in averting the economic, social, and political disruptions that can occur if supplies are interrupted [41]. Energy insecurity can precipitate a loss in welfare as a result of the physical unavailability of energy or prices that are volatile and not competitive [41, 42]. Due to the interdependence that characterizes today's energy markets, considerable scope exists for countries to coordinate their energy strategies to reduce their vulnerabilities to energy shocks and improve their overall energy security. Some measures that are currently being used to improve energy security include:

i. *Investments in energy resources and infrastructure*: Countries and/or regions can improve their energy security by undertaking investments that promote exploration, extraction, processing, transportation, and marketing of energy resources. One of the objectives of these initiatives is to upgrade existing energy infrastructure and develop new transmission infrastructure that is crucial to energy security. This is occurring in several regions such as the United States, Africa, and the Caspian Basin. In the United States, for example, previously restrictive regulations have been amended to allow offshore drilling in the Gulf of Mexico, horizontal drilling, hydraulic fracturing, and the drilling for oil and natural gas in the Arctic National Wildlife Refuge in Alaska. These measures have resulted in a substantial increase in oil and natural gas production in the United States and reduced the country's dependence on energy imports. Pipeline projects from the Caspian Basin have also contributed to increasing the supply of oil and natural gas to Europe and Asia. In Africa, the energy infrastructure projects that have recently been commissioned include the Grand Inga Dam in the Democratic Republic of Congo that will produce about 40,000 MW of electricity when completed; the Rusumo Falls Hydroelectric Project in Rwanda that aims to supply about 80 MW of power to Rwanda, Tanzania and Burundi; the Lake Turkana wind power project in Kenya that will provide the country's national grid with about 300 MW of clean power; and, the Jasper Power project in the Northern Cape of South Africa that aims to generate 18 GW of clean energy by 2030. The successful completion of these and similar projects will increase the overall energy supply and enhance energy security.

ii. *Investments in energy efficiency*: Energy efficiency is an important instrument for stemming the growth in energy demand, providing households and firms with cost savings due to reduced energy use, and reducing the emissions of greenhouse gases [43, 44]. According to the International Energy Agency, energy efficiency is the world's most available, secure and affordable energy resource that every government has the power to exploit for widespread benefit [44]. To the extent that energy efficiency actions such as retrofitting homes, adopting more stringent building codes, increasing the fuel economy of vehicles, and adopting more productive technologies in industries reduce energy demand and consumption, they contribute towards the goal of energy security [45]. It is estimated that between 2000 and 2017, improvements in energy efficiency saved an additional 37 exajoules of final energy use in the IEA countries and other major economies and that globally, over this period, efficiency improvements prevented about 12% more energy use [46]. The fact that energy efficiency potential is vast and has not been fully utilized in many countries implies that it is a strategy that can be cost-effectively used to improve energy security. This will entail identifying the barriers to the implementation of energy efficiency programs and addressing these barriers through appropriate policy actions [43].

iii. *Energy diversification*: Countries can enhance their energy security by diversifying the types of energy carriers that their economies depend on and also the sources of their energy supply. Kruyt et al. [17] regard diversification as critical to energy security because the increasing global demand for energy can over time lead to the depletion of currently known energy resources. Yergin [6] notes that energy diversification enhances energy security by allowing societies to absorb shocks in one energy input by increasing the use of other energy inputs. Li [47] asserts that diversifying a country's energy system is vital not only for mitigating the risks that arise from over-reliance on fossil fuels, but also for achieving the goal of sustainable development. Trinidad and Tobago are an example of a country whose primary energy supply is not diverse and consists of 72.3% natural gas and 27.7% crude oil. Canada, in contrast, has a diverse energy mix consisting of natural gas, oil, coal, hydropower, nuclear and others and is therefore much less prone to shortages and price shocks because it is unlikely that these systems would all fail at the same time. Having multiple sources of energy enables countries to continue without disruption if one of the energy sources failed. Over the medium to long-term, Trinidad and Tobago can diversify their energy mix by developing and harnessing their vast potential for wind and solar power.

iv. *Technological innovation*: Technological innovation, like energy efficiency, is a valuable instrument that countries can use to mitigate climate change and enhance their overall energy security. Kim [48] cites Germany and

Japan as examples of countries that are not well endowed with vast oil reserves, but which have invested heavily in alternative energy technologies especially in the transportation sector. These technologies include fuel cells and electric and hybrid vehicles that are increasingly being adopted as a response to the high gasoline prices. Lin and Chen [49] and Lin and Zhu [50] argue that technological innovation is key in developing renewable energy and promoting the transition to a low-carbon economy. Denholm and Hand [51] advance a similar argument and assert that increased grid flexibility and energy storage are critical innovations that are required to achieve high penetration of wind and solar energy. They further claim that in the United States, the limits of wind and solar energy are not resource based; that wind and solar resources are significantly greater than the total electric demand; and, that the primary technical challenge is the resource intermittency that can be addressed through technical innovations that enable energy storage.

The availability of vast supplies of fossil energy resources implies that their increased utilization is a viable strategy that can be used to meet the rising demand for energy and enhance energy security. This option is however not favoured by policy makers who claim that it is likely to increase emissions of carbon dioxide and undermine efforts to mitigate climate change [52]. Carbon capture and storage is a technological innovation that can permit an increase in the use of fossil fuels but curtail the release of stationary carbon dioxide emissions into the atmosphere [53]. According to the IEA [54], more investment needs to be made in carbon capture and storage that has been demonstrated to be a low-cost technological pathway that can help achieve deep decarbonization, promote greater energy security, support diversity of power generation and enhance economic prosperity and employment.

v. *Market and institutional reforms*: Several countries are currently reforming their energy markets to improve security of supply by incentivising investments in secure, low-carbon energy sources; improving efficiency and productivity; supporting cost-effective integration of renewable energy sources; and, improving affordability for consumers [55–57]. Some of the issues that these reforms aim to address are: inadequate electricity generation and distribution infrastructure when electricity demand is growing rapidly [55, 57]; underutilization of cheap resources and overutilization of expensive resources; unnecessary curtailment of renewable energy; existence of barriers to minimizing the cost of power due to inability of energy distribution companies to access all available power generation and the associated marginal costs; lack of flexibility in the energy system; heavy and restrictive regulations that impose costs and hinder innovation; and distortions in energy markets. Examples of reforms that various countries have implemented to address these issues include: liberalization of the downstream gas market in Egypt to end government monopoly, increase competition, and attract foreign direct investment to the energy sector [58]; deregulation of energy prices in China to optimize energy allocation, improve energy efficiency, promote the penetration of renewable energy, and induce energy-saving technologies and innovations [59]; and, expansion of cross-border electricity cooperation and trade through establishment of regional electricity grids in South Asia [60]. Where reforms have been properly designed and implemented, they have increased competition in energy markets, reduced energy prices to consumers, stimulated technological and structural change, increased the share of renewable energy in the energy mix, increased the reliability of the energy system, reduced power outages, increased investment in the energy sector, and improved energy security [16].

5. Conclusions and implications

Energy resources play a critical role in economic growth and human wellbeing and will continue to be a key concern to policy makers in both developed and developing countries. How energy is produced and used will also continue to be of national and global concern because greenhouse gas emissions from these processes are the primary cause of global warming and climate change. The rapid growth in the demand for energy in recent years due to robust economic expansion, population growth, and new uses of energy is a major challenge that requires policy actions to ensure that energy users have access to reliable, affordable, and secure energy supplies. It is a problematic situation to countries that are not endowed with abundant energy resources and must rely on energy imports. There are however several strategies that countries can implement individually or jointly to improve their energy security. First, agricultural by-products and crop residues such as maize stalks, rice straw, cattle dung, molasses and bagasse can be harnessed and used to produce energy products such as methane which can be used for cooking, heating and lighting [61]. These processes can also be used to produce alcohol which can be used to blend automotive fossil fuels. Energy security can be positively impacted by these measures because they expand the supplies of available energy resources and reduce the demand for conventional energy. Second, countries can increase their energy security by harnessing renewable energy such as wind, solar, and geothermal energy and integrating them into the energy system. This alternative holds considerable promise particularly in regions such as North Africa and the Middle East. Third, through investments in energy efficiency, countries can reduce their demand for energy and enhance their energy security. This can be accomplished through more stringent building codes, market penetration of hybrid and electric cars that have greater fuel economy, and real-time pricing of electricity. Fourth, energy security can be greatly enhanced by improving the performance of energy markets through deep reforms and institutional changes. If properly designed and implemented, the reforms can reduce wastage, incentivise private sector investment in energy generation, increase competition in energy markets reducing the prices to consumers, and improve overall efficiency. Fifth, global energy security can be enhanced through international cooperation on energy issues and the promotion of regional energy trade. Such trade will be a win-win outcome for both exporters and importers of energy.

Author details

Collins Ayoo
Department of Economics, Carleton University, Ottawa, Ontario, Canada

*Address all correspondence to: collins.ayoo@carleton.ca

References

[1] Pode R. Addressing India's energy security and options for decreasing energy dependency. Renewable and Sustainable Energy Reviews. 2010;**14**: 3014-3022

[2] Bompard E, Carpignano A, Erriquez M, Grosso D, Pession M, Profumo F. National energy security assessment in a geopolitical perspective. Energy. 2017;**130**:144-154

[3] Warr BS, Ayre RU. Evidence of causality between the quantity and quality of energy consumption and economic growth. Energy. 2010;**35**(4): 1688-1693

[4] Global Energy Institute (GEI). International index of energy security risk: Assessing risk in a global energy market. 2018. Available at: https://www.globalenergyinstitute.org/energy-security-risk-index

[5] Klare MT. The futile pursuit of "energy security" by military force. The Brown Journal of World Affairs. 2007; **13**(2):139-153

[6] Yergin D. Ensuring energy security. Foreign Affairs. 2006;**85**(2):69-82

[7] Richter PM, Holz F. All quiet on the eastern front? Disruption scenarios of Russian natural gas supply to Europe. Energy Policy. 2015;**80**:177-189

[8] Bohi DR, Toman MA. Energy security: Externalities and policies. Energy Policy. 1993;**21**(11):1093-1109

[9] Bohi DR, Toman MA. The Economics of Energy Security. Deventer: Kluwer Academic Publishers; 1996

[10] Cherp A, Jewell J. The three perspectives on energy security: Intellectual history, disciplinary roots and the potential for integration. Current Opinion in Environmental Sustainability. 2011;**3**(4):202-212

[11] Winzer C. Conceptualizing energy security. Energy Policy. 2012;**46**:36-48

[12] Andrews CJ. Energy security as a rationale for governmental action. IEEE Technology and Society Magazine. 2005;**24**(2):16-25

[13] Jun E, Kim W, Chang H. The analysis of security cost for different energy sources. Applied Energy. 2009; **86**(10):1894-1901

[14] Intharak N, Julay JH, Nakanishi S, Matsumoto T, Sahid EJM, Aquino AGO, et al. A Quest for Energy Security in the 21st Century. Tokyo, Japan: Asia Pacific Energy Research Centre; 2007

[15] World Commission on Environment and Development (WCED). Our Common Future. New York: Oxford University Press; 1987

[16] Grubb M, Butler L, Twomey P. Diversity and security in UK Electricity generation: The influence of low-carbon objectives. Energy Policy. 2006;**34**(18): 4050-4062

[17] Kruyt B, van Vuuren DP, de Vries HJM, Groenenberg H. Indicators for energy security. Energy Policy. 2009;**37**(6):2166-2181

[18] Sovacool BK. Reassessing energy security and the trans-ASEAN natural gas pipeline network in Southeast Asia. Pacific Affairs. 2009;**82**:467-486

[19] Sovacool BK. The Routledge Handbook of Energy Security. London: Routledge; 2010

[20] Sovacool BK. Evaluating energy security in the Asia Pacific: Towards a more comprehensive approach. Energy Policy. 2011;**39**(11):7472-7479

[21] Sovacool BK. An international assessment of energy security performance. Ecological Economics. 2013;**88**:148-158

[22] Sovacool BK, Brown MA. Competing dimensions of energy security: An international review. Annual Review of Environment and Resources. 2010;**35**:77-108

[23] Sovacool BK, Mukherjee I. Conceptualizing and measuring energy security: A synthesized approach. Energy. 2011;**36**(8):5343-5355

[24] Sovacool BK, Mukherjee I, Drupady IM, D'Agostino AL. Evaluating energy security performance from 1990 to 2010 for eighteen countries. Energy. 2011;**36**(10):5846-5853

[25] Brown MA, Sovacool BK. Climate Change and Global Energy Security: Technology and Policy Options. Cambridge, MA: MIT Press; 2011

[26] Badea AC, Rocco SCM, Tarantola S, Bolado R. Composite indicators for security of energy supply using ordered weighted averaging. Reliability Engineering and System Safety. 2011; **96**(6):651-662

[27] Brown MA, Wang Y, Sovacool BK, D'Agostino AL. Forty years of energy security trends: A comparative assessment of 22 industrialized countries. Energy Research & Social Science. 2014;**4**:64-77

[28] Asia Pacific Energy Research Centre (APERC). A Quest for Energy Security in the 21st Century: Resources and Constraints. Japan: Tokyo; 2007

[29] van den Bremer TS, van der Ploeg F. Managing and harnessing volatile oil windfalls. IMF Economic Review. 2013; **61**(1):130-167

[30] BP Statistical Review of World Energy. 2018

[31] International Energy Agency (IEA). Global Gas Security Review 2018: Meeting Challenges in a Fast Changing Market. Paris: OECD/IEA; 2018. Available from: https://webstore.iea.org/global-gas-security-review-2018

[32] International Energy Agency (IEA). World Energy Outlook. Paris: OECD/IEA; 2018

[33] Neelawela UD, Selvanathan EA, Wagner LD. Global measure of electricity security: A composite index approach. Energy Economics. 2019;**81**: 433-453

[34] Lesbirel S. Diversification and energy security risks: The Japanese case. Japanese Journal of Political Science. 2004;**5**(1):1-22

[35] Hasanov M. An analysis of economic benefits of the Southern Gas Corridor. Energy Sources, Part B: Economics, Planning, and Policy. 2016;**11**(11): 999-1005

[36] Morningstar R. The legacy of the Southern Gas Corridor. Turkish Policy Quarterly. 2018;**17**(3):39-44

[37] Chen X, Huang H, Khanna M, Önal H. Alternative transportation fuel standards: Welfare effects and climate benefits. Journal of Environmental Economics and Management. 2014; **67**(3):241-257

[38] Flynn PC. Commercializing an alternate vehicle fuel: Lessons learned from natural gas for vehicles. Energy Policy. 2002;**30**(7):613-619

[39] Jansen J, van der Welle A. The role of regulation in integrating renewable energy: The EU electricity sector. In: Goldthau A, editor. The Handbook of Global Energy Policy. Wiley-Blackwell; 2013. pp. 322-339

[40] Barbose G, Wiser R, Heeter J, Mai T, Bird L, Bolingera M, et al.

A retrospective analysis of benefits and impacts of U.S. renewable portfolio standards. Energy Policy. 2016;**96**: 645-660

[41] Barton B, Redgwell C, Rønne A, Zillman DN. Energy Security: Managing Risk in a Dynamic Legal and Regulatory Environment. Oxford, UK: Oxford University Press; 2004

[42] Höök M, Tang X. Depletion of fossil fuels and anthropogenic climate change—A review. Energy Policy. 2013;**52**: 797-809

[43] Ayoo C. The role of efficiency in energy policy. International Journal of Environment and Sustainable Development. 2016;**15**(4):423-449

[44] International Energy Agency (IEA). Energy Efficiency 2017. Paris: OECD/IEA; 2017

[45] Nepal R, Jamasb T, Tisdell CA. Market-related reforms and increased energy efficiency in transition countries: Empirical evidence. Applied Economics. 2014;**46**(33):4125-4136

[46] International Energy Agency (IEA). Energy Efficiency 2018. Paris: OECD/IEA; 2018

[47] Li X. Diversification and localization of energy systems for sustainable development and energy security. Energy Policy. 2005;**33**(17):2237-2243

[48] Kim JE. Energy security and climate change: How oil endowment influences alternative vehicle innovation. Energy Policy. 2014;**66**: 400-410

[49] Lin B, Chen Y. Does electricity price matter for innovation in renewable energy technologies in China? Energy Economics. 2019;**78**:259-266

[50] Lin B, Zhu J. The role of renewable energy technological innovation on climate change: Empirical evidence from China. Science of the Total Environment. 2019;**659**:1505-1512

[51] Denholm P, Hand M. Grid flexibility and storage required to achieve very high penetration of variable renewable electricity. Energy Policy. 2011;**39**(3): 1817-1830

[52] Hoffert MI. Farewell to fossil fuels? Science. 2010;**329**(5997):1292-1294

[53] Mikunda T, Kober T, de Coninck H, Bazilian M, Rösler H, van der Zwaan B. Designing policy for deployment of CCS in industry. Climate Policy. 2014;**14**(5): 665-676

[54] International Energy Agency (IEA). Five Keys to Unlock CCS Investment. Paris: OECD/IEA; 2017

[55] Department of Energy and Climate Change (DECC). Electricity Market Reform: Policy Overview. 2012. Available at: https://assets.publishing.service.gov.uk/government/uploads/system/uploads/attachment_data/file/65634/7090-electricity-market-reform-policy-overview-.pdf

[56] International Energy Agency (IEA). Electricity Market Reform: An IEA Handbook, Energy Market Reform. Paris: OECD/IEA; 2000

[57] Patel D. India kick-starts wholesale electricity market reforms. 2019. Available at: https://energypost.eu/india-kick-starts-wholesale-energy-market-reforms/

[58] Elshazly M, Khodeir S. Legislative reforms in the Egyptian energy sector to liberalize the natural gas market. Journal of World Energy Law and Business. 2018;**11**:354-359

[59] Fan Y, Liao H, Wei Y. Can market oriented economic reforms contribute to energy efficiency improvement?

Evidence from China. Energy Policy. 2007;**35**(4):2287-2295

[60] Timilsina GR, Toman M. Potential gains from expanding regional electricity trade in South Asia. Energy Economics. 2016;**60**:6-14

[61] Ayoo C, Bonti-Ankomah S. Economic impacts of value addition to agricultural byproducts. In: Simpson BK, Aryee ANA, Toldra F, editors. Byproducts from Agriculture and Fisheries: Adding Value for Food, Feed, Pharma, and Fuels. Hoboken, NJ: Wiley; 2020. pp. 685-698

Section 2

Energy Policy

Chapter 3

Energy Savings Analysis of a Recommended Residential Air Conditioning Incentive Program in Saudi Arabia

Faisal Fahad Al-Musa

Abstract

Over the past couple of decades, the kingdom's annual per capita electricity consumption has been steadily growing by around 7%. One of the key causes for such a high growth is the intensive use of non-energy-efficient equipment, which was dominating the Saudi market. In 2017, the residential sector consumed around 143 TWh, which represents around 48% of the country's total electricity consumption. The aim of this study is to assess the feasibility of an air conditioning incentive program for citizens from energy and economic sides. This chapter is a detailed study where program gains from energy and economic standpoints were based on substituting participants' old air conditioning units with new units that are better in performance. The proposed program was designed over an 8-year period with three scenarios where the government will take care of all the capital cost, 75%, and none of the capital cost in these scenarios. The results of this study indicated that an accumulated savings of up to 17.11 TWh by 2025 with NPVs above $13 billion can be achieved in all scenarios. Moreover, it was estimated that the program will add an average of $0.5 billion per year to the kingdom's GDP over the duration of the program.

Keywords: energy efficiency, energy savings, air conditioning, HVAC, subsidy program, incentive program, residential, Saudi Arabia, KSA

1. Introduction

The Kingdom of Saudi Arabia is one of the nations that are blessed with plenty of energy resources, specifically fossil fuels in the form of oil and gas. In addition, it has a huge potential for renewable application which has not been leashed at full capacity yet. This wealth of energy resource was one of the main factors to have and maintain low energy prices for decades in all the sectors, namely, industrial, transportation, or buildings. For instance, the average electricity price was around $0.03/KWh for long time which is considered one of the lowest worldwide. Over the past years, the kingdom's per capita electricity consumption was rising swiftly with an average annual rise of 7% where the year 2000 electricity consumption was 5640 KWh per capita compared to a world's average of 2384 and the 2014 numbers were 9444 KWh per capita compared to the global average of 3127 as per the World Bank statistics.

The buildings sector is considered one of the main energy consumers in the kingdom with a total of nearly 9 million electrically connected customers in 2017, with the bulk, 7.1 million, being residential customers. As per the Saudi Electricity and Cogeneration Regulatory Authority (ECRA), the residential sector consumed nearly 143 TWh, which represents 48% of the country's electricity consumption. The high residential energy consumption is projected to keep rising in the future attributing to a number of factors among which are the expected population increase, the low energy prices despite of the recent rise, and the vibrant infrastructure expansion under the kingdom's 2030 vision.

Such existence of low energy prices coupled with the absence of stringent standards, building code enforcement, and standards and labeling (S&L) programs led to wasteful pattern of energy consumption among citizens which resulted in depleting the kingdom's natural resource at higher rates than normal compared to international records.

The Saudi government realized this fact and decided to change the existing situation. Hence, Saudi policy makers acknowledged the fact that energy efficiency and conservation shall be set as one of the nation's top priorities for the national energy security. This was apparent via inaugurating the Saudi Energy Efficiency Program (SEEP) activities to help in jump-starting the energy efficiency efforts within the kingdom by designing a comprehensive integrated framework consisting of several key pillars and enablers. In order to ensure sustainability, the Saudi Energy Efficiency Center (SEEC) was established in 2010 aiming for rationalizing the production and consumption of energy in all sectors in order to ensure the kingdom's efficiency along with unifying efforts in this field among governmental bodies and nongovernmental entities as well. The center's mission is to preserve the national wealth of energy sources in a manner that promotes development and the national economy and achieves the lowest possible levels of consumptions. The efforts made by the government since the inception of the energy efficiency program had a great and clear impact from different aspects in each and every sector. Zooming into the buildings sector, the efforts were obvious by completing several milestones including updating the Saudi Building Code along with introducing several Minimum Energy Performance Standards (MEPS) for a number of equipment, enforcement of insulation standards for new buildings, introducing S&L programs for different appliances, and much more.

The aforementioned efforts helped the market to be in a better situation by slowly getting rid of less efficient equipment along with changing the mindset of citizens to be mindful of their energy consumption patterns. Nevertheless, in order to further normalize the uncontrolled demand for building energy, it is vital that more energy-efficient improvement opportunities be assessed and progressively executed. One of these opportunities is to introduce an incentive program for the existing fleet of air conditioners with low energy efficiency ratings especially in the residential sector as the main consumer within the buildings sector of Saudi Arabia which is the topic of this chapter. However, before going into the details of the proposal, some light need to be shed on the purpose of such programs, the appropriate time for their introduction in a market, their implementation mechanism, and finally the main challenges or barriers that might face such programs. This will be detailed in the literature review section.

With regard to air conditioning in Saudi Arabia, The Saudi Standards, Metrology and Quality Organization (SASO) have done great efforts in developing the SASO 2663 standard for Energy Labeling and Minimum Energy Performance Requirements for Air-Conditioners (phase 1, 2013; and phase 2, 2015). Now it is time to start developing an incentive program that would help not only in reducing electric consumption and summer peak demand but would correspondingly avoid pricey power outages in peak hot summer months and cut greenhouse gases (GHG) emissions. Moreover, it would aid in supporting SASO 2663 for a further shift in efficiency levels.

2. Literature review

This section will provide an overview of the policy frameworks and program designs that will be helpful as a preparation to the reader into the proposed subject of residential air conditioning incentive program for the kingdom of Saudi Arabia. In addition, some light will be shed on energy analysis approaches. Finally, techno-economic assessment will be reviewed with focus on net present value.

Incentive programs usually complement standards and labeling procedures by speeding up market permeation of more energy-efficient products than required by current standards in place and by also preparing the market for further stringent future standards requirements. Incentives can be focused at several points in the appliance's supply chain; a precise point may be more effective than another subject to different factors including, but not limited to, the maturity of the technology and market permeation. Financial incentive packages have larger impact when they are focused toward highly efficient technologies that have a smaller market share, and those program designs will be going to depend on market barriers addressed, targeted equipment, and local market situation. Therefore, it is safe to say that there is no specific one program design that is inherently better than the other. The key here is to design an effective program by implementing a comprehensive understanding of the market and the identification of the vital local complications to the penetration of energy-efficient technologies [1].

Several barriers contribute in discouraging consumers from investing in energy-efficient equipment. These barriers may include absence of information, split incentives (between landlords and renters), and lack of energy-efficient equipment on the market [2–4]. One of the most major barriers that policy makers detect is the fairly higher up-front prices of efficient products. Usually these costs discourage potential buyers even when investments seem to be in consumers' interest (i.e., cost-effective over the lifetime of the equipment). Consumers set great value on instant savings and profoundly discount future savings [5, 6]. Additionally and as they might not be able to simply evaluate future savings, consumers tend to have less confidence in expected paybacks. Consequently, consumers regularly purchase the cheapest available options. Many incentive programs have been established worldwide to address these barriers and speed up the penetration of efficient equipment [6].

2.1 Policy frameworks

The classical policy frameworks in which incentive programs are developed are either (1) government rollouts with fund raised through taxes or (2) compulsory savings goals agreed for energy providers (i.e., utilities) to decrease their customers' energy consumption. Incentive programs, over the history, have been implemented by different governments for one main purpose, and that is to support long-run growing domestic clean product market [7].

Examples of compulsory savings goal schemes include those exist in Brazil, some Australian states, South Korea, China, India, and South Africa [8, 9]. In Australia, New South Wales State implemented the world's first obligatory GHG emissions exchange scheme in 2003, in which electricity GHG emissions are capped each year [7]. Since 1998, the Brazilian power regulatory authority, ANEEL, mandated utilities to invest at least 0.5 percent of the net revenues in energy efficiency programs. The Brazilian Congress necessitates that around half of these funds must be spent on energy efficiency measures targeting low-income households [10].

In India, the Maharashtra Electricity Regulatory Commission (MERC) introduced a public benefit type of electricity charge on utilities where funds are used to finance energy efficiency and renewable energy programs. In 2005, MERC requested utility companies to use these resources to start compact fluorescent light (CFL) programs in Mumbai's residential sector [11]. As can be seen from such examples, governments are developing policy frameworks in order to increase the role of energy efficiency.

2.2 Funding sources

Financial incentive programs are capital-intensive in nature, involving not only administration costs but costs of financial incentives for every participating appliance unit. In general, government-sponsored incentive programs are financed through government budgets funded by taxpayers. Developing countries governments can pursue monetary support from international financial institutions such as the World Bank. For example, India's Super-Efficient Equipment Program for electric fans is supported by the Clean Technology Fund, which is administered by World Bank [12].

Earmarked taxes can also finance energy efficiency programs. For instance, South Korea introduced a 5 to 6.5 percent tax on energy consuming appliances where the revenues from the tax were used to subsidize the procurement of efficient products by low-income households [13]. These types of policies are known as a feebate (a portmanteau of "fee" and "rebate") which is basically a fee on products with low energy efficiencies that is utilized in order to be directed as rebates on better-performing products [1].

Under the current budget limitations that the government of Saudi Arabia is facing nowadays, the feebate policy could be an appropriate vehicle to implement the proposed air conditioning incentive program.

2.3 Program designs

The major challenge of incentive program design is to accomplish robust market transformation [14, 15]. Programs need to be customized to address different stages of energy-efficient products' market diffusion to increase the products' penetration through a sustainable manner. In general, the diffusion of efficient technologies follows an S curve [16]. At the beginning, limited early participants will be willing to take risk in purchasing expensive new technologies, thus market diffusion is considered small at this stage. After the technology has been proven, the technology's market penetration rates rise faster. After that market penetration of technology levels off, only "idlers" will remain unwilling to implement new technologies [1].

Standard and labeling (S&L) programs are normally considered the first of policy intrusions to alter the market of a specific product. S&L programs approve technologies based on their energy performance and hence take out energy intensive technologies from a specific market, which ultimately results in raising efficiency levels. Incentive programs are better implemented if S&L programs are in place. A typical cycle of market conversion starts with energy-intensive products which are removed from a market by minimum energy performance standards (MEPS). Then, existing equipment efficiency is elevated utilizing energy inducement programs. Those inducement programs focus on highly efficient products with best-in-class identified equipment by the S&L programs. It is worth mentioning that programs focusing on consumers are called "downstream" programs, programs focusing on distributors and retailers are often called "midstream," and finally those focusing on manufacturers of products are usually called "upstream" [1].

In Saudi Arabia, the standard for air conditioners (ACs) was already issued and enforced since September 2013, and now it is time for incentive programs. The standard is SASO 2663: 2104 titled “Energy Labeling and Minimum Energy Performance Requirements for Air-Conditioners” and has the requirements presented in the table below:

Air conditioner appliance type	Cooling capacity (CC) limit (Btu/h)	Mandatory EER phase 1: 7 September 2013	Mandatory EER phase 1: 7 September 2013	Mandatory EER phase 2: 1 January 2015	Mandatory EER phase 2: 1 January 2015
	At testing conditions T1 (35°C)	T1 (35°C)	T3 (46°C)	T1 (35°C)	T3 (46°C)
Window type	CC <18,000	8.5	6.12	9.8	7.06
	18,000 ≤ CC < 24,000	8.5	6.12	9.7	6.98
	CC ≥ 24,000	8.5	6.12	8.5	6.12
Split type and other types	All capacities	9.5	6.84	11.5	8.28

Incentives raise equipment desire and consequently market a shift toward more efficient equipment which leads to price reduction over time and hence more production of such equipment by manufacturers. The increase in fleets’ energy efficiency, realized through inducement programs, will be then paved by applying more stringent standards which will lead to endless sequence of improvements. This twirl can be continual as technology advances in developing more energy-efficient products. To further advance the penetration rate, further programs can be introduced such as awareness programs and awards [1].

In other countries which have weaker standards and S&L programs in place, incentive programs can aid to push for more efficient product penetration. Incentive programs can also be used as a vehicle to make more stringent standards acceptable to the public as well as manufacturers in a specific country. Furthermore, inducement programs affect people’s buying choices, and if implemented with the existence of an S&L program, they will both definitely work in harmony to aid in enlightening citizens about the advantages of the more energy-efficient equipment. The availability of a consumer partial refund program is by itself a sign of the great value of the labeling program in place. Partial refund programs are usually connected with better energy-efficient units. Caution: when designing an incentive program, the program should address the issue of free ridership. Free riders are those who take advantage of incentives yet would have purchased efficient technologies even without the incentives [1].

Gold and Nadel settled that incentive programs should last for a limited time, typically around 5 years, since incentives become less effective over time [17]. Rosenberg and Hoefgen concluded that various harmonized market interventions over an extended period of time are more likely to affect the behavior of market actors than programs that include a single intervention during a short period of time [14]. With time, a program can raise the overall efficiency of the units on the market. Gold and Nadel found that the refrigerator tax credit upstream program in the USA has been essentially successful as each extension of the program pressed the efficiency standard higher so that next set of incentives would further increase the energy saved. One of the main reasons for the program’s success was vigorous stakeholder engagement and education with regard to how to participate in the program [17].

2.4 Incentive beneficiary

Partial refunds can be delivered in any point in the equipment supply chain, but typically they are provided to end consumers. The decision shall be made based on specific market's characteristics and obstacles. For example, product manufacturers will be targeted if the production of more energy-efficient products is needed, while distributors might be targeted if efficient equipment accessibility is the main obstacle in that specific market [1]. In this chapter's proposal, end customers are targeted, and hence it is of a downstream-type program.

Downstream inducements have the benefit of increasing buyers' acceptance of energy-efficient units, which has helpful spillover effects (i.e., the purchase of energy-efficient units by nonparticipants in the program due to the enhanced knowledge about the benefits of energy efficiency). The presence of a refund by itself is a signal and could in some cases have greater impact than the cash amount. Furthermore, downstream-type programs have a unique feature where they can be easily directed to a particular group of the society such as low-income households. However, a drawback of such programs could be the massive operation costs required in delivering refunds to big numbers of beneficiaries on individual basis [1].

2.5 Evaluation

Programs and policies are not usually thoroughly evaluated. Governments do not at all times allocate money and time to assess their programs in details. Moreover, a certain program could have various goals, which can be wide-ranging, especially when they incorporate research and development elements; this complicates evaluation of the program's success. Evaluation of rate-funded programs is more likely to be performed more scientifically as a necessary input to plan for upcoming resource investment, and impact evaluations are normally part of the development of these programs [18].

2.6 Examples of downstream programs

The typical fiscal tools used for downstream programs along with consumer reward points and replacement programs are briefly described below.

2.6.1 Downstream fiscal instruments

Fiscal instruments that include income/sales tax reduction are popular incentives applied by governments. Since 2005, France has had an effective tax credit (tax credits reduce the taxes the consumer pays, whereas tax deductions lower the consumer's taxable income). As of 2010, more than 6.2 million households had benefited from this French tax credit [19]. Tax credits can be applied for the purchase of efficient boilers, windows, heat pumps, and even renewable energy equipment. Since 2007, the Italian government has offered a tax deduction of 55 percent for the replacement of heating, ventilation, and air conditioning (HVAC) systems with more efficient units and for the cost of other home efficiency improvements as well. Until December 2010, the program included a tax deduction of 20 percent for the replacement of old refrigerators. A tax deduction of 50 percent was newly added for the replacement of white goods including refrigerators, dryers, washers, ovens, freezers, and gas cookers [20].

2.6.2 Consumer reward points

South Korea and Japan have applied subsidies in the form of reward points to incentivize consumers to select efficient technologies. This approach aims at promoting low-carbon lifestyles by encouraging consumer responsibility and awareness [1].

2.6.3 Replacement programs

Replacement programs (i.e., premature retirement and direct install) replace wasteful products before their useful estimated life is ended with more energy-efficient ones. Such programs help in decreasing energy use by inspiring the placement of efficient products and confirming that non-efficient ones are taken away from the market [1]. Mexico's PNSEE has replaced large numbers of old appliances. The program offers government-funded subsidies to households in order to replace their old refrigerators and air conditioners with more efficient ones. The subsidies cover a percentage of the price of the new equipment and the costs for removing the old one. To receive the subsidy, households must surrender working refrigerators and air conditioners that must be 10 years old or older [21].

2.7 Energy analysis

Approaches of energy savings vary between countries, and they have a major effect on results. For instance, in Europe the savings are commonly based on lifetime energy saving which covers accumulated savings over the life of the equipment over the program duration, while the California Public Utilities Commission objective is based on yearly energy savings gathered over a period of 3 years [1].

Also, diverse methods are utilized to estimate net savings from incentive programs. An inducement program's net energy savings are usually the percentage of savings related only to the program itself. Those gross savings do not include the savings coming from the freerides who are contributors that will purchase efficient equipment without the availability of the program. Yet, it includes savings from participants who were encouraged to purchase efficient products as a result from the program's impact on that market that are usually referred to as spillovers. Furthermore, gross savings does not include savings resulting from other programs such as existing standards/codes, S&L programs, other monetary inducement programs, and of course external events such as economic recessions/growths. Usually gross savings calculation is not easy considering the existence of different bodies within the country offering several other different monetary programs for the same equipment. A final concern that should be accounted for is the increase in energy consumption that happens within the program participants as a result of the decrease of their energy bills which is a phenomenon typically referred to as rebound effect. Continuous evaluation and assessments are important and shall be performed regularly by governments to keep program administrators up to speed and aware of possible drawbacks that incentive programs might face and how they can be fixed [1].

Moreover and before going into energy analysis and savings quantification in this chapter, it is vital to understand what an energy system is. Scott wrote a paper about "the energy system" and defined it from sources to services where services are basically what people wants and sources are what nature provides as can be seen in the figure below [22].

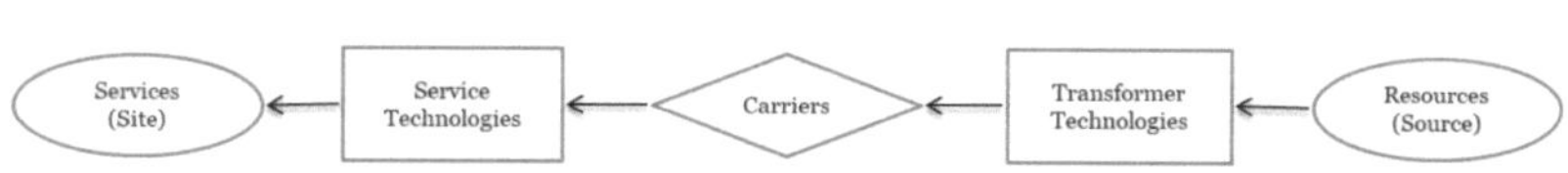

Sources, transformer technologies, and carriers together identify the energy sector. Hence, it can be understood that the energy sector is only a part of the energy system [22]. As we are evaluating air conditioning incentive program in this study, the below graph describes the energy system, as per Scott, of a space cooling service in Saudi Arabia.

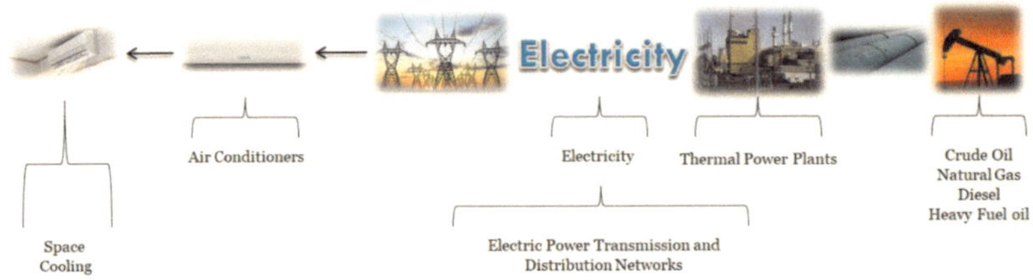

In this chapter the focus will be on final or site energy savings quantification mainly not the primary energy saved. This is why it was important for the reader from a comprehension point of view to be provided with a glimpse of site-to-source energy systems. Since the proposal is about Saudi Arabia, it would be also useful to shed some light on Al-Musa et al.'s [23] efforts in implementing Scott's concept of energy systems to the Saudi electricity and LPG systems for cooking and water heating applications where they quantified the efficiency of the system by using the following formula [23]:

$$\eta\text{System} = \eta\text{Extraction}^{*}\eta\text{Transportation}^{*} \eta\text{Transformer Technology}^{*}\eta T\&\text{D}^{*}\eta\text{ServiceTechnology}. \quad (1)$$

They found out that the Saudi electric system efficiency from source to service is around 20 and 23% for cooking and water heating applications, respectively [23]. If a model to be developed for the space cooling applications is using the same formula, the efficiency of the service technology needs to be changed to consider window and split units' efficiencies. However, this is outside the scope of this chapter.

Another example from a developing nation is the efforts described by McNeil and Michael (2005) in their research where they studied the possible benefits from improved energy efficiency of key electrical products in India. The objective of the project was to assess the benefits which cost-effective enhancements in energy efficiency may get to developing nations. The project focused on four appliances among which are the air conditioning units. The life cycle cost analysis methodology was used in this project along with identifying the country's energy and environmental impacts in an attempt to offer through estimations of the possible returns of appliances energy efficiency programs in India [24].

The proposal in this chapter was analyzed with focus on energy efficiency and energy analysis. However, it is worth mentioning that several other researches focus also on exergy efficiencies and exergy analysis. Tolga Taner (2105) mentioned in his paper that energy analysis may be clarified with an exergy analysis where exergy is defined as the available energy [25]. Also, exergy could be defined as the available work or quality of energy. It basically quantifies the capability of a source to create useful work. Hence, exergy is considered a thermodynamic unit that offers a numerical value to the energy quality [25].

Muller et al. emphasized that exergy analysis is an essential tool which can be utilized in order to design and also operate an energy system. They also stressed on the importance of exergy analysis due to its significance for whole system exergy destruction [26].

Although very important, exergy efficiencies and analysis are outside the scope of this chapter, and it focuses mainly on energy efficiencies and energy analysis.

2.8 Techno-economic assessment (TEA)

This chapter attempted to quantify the energy savings and the associated economic feasibility from a proposed incentive program where several assumptions and estimations are needed and were utilized. Maximilian Lauer (2008) described several techno-economic assessment (TEA) methods among which are the net present value (NPV), annuity method, net cash flow table, and internal rate of return where he referred to the NPV method as the most common method utilized by the majority of professional practitioners of techno-economic assessment [27]. In this chapter the net present value (NPV) (discounted cash flow) will be used as one of the techno-economic assessment (TEA) methods where the net present value of each year will be discounted to year zero by the discount rate by means of the following formula [27]:

$$NPVn = \frac{NFC}{(1+d)^n} \tag{2}$$

Hence, the NPV of the project (i.e., NPV_{total}) will be the total of the discounted cash flow for each year over the project period [27]:

$$NPVtotal = \sum_{1}^{n} NPVn \tag{3}$$

Maximilian recommended performing sensitivity analysis to investigate the effect of input parameters on the results which will be performed in this chapter. Sensitivity analysis shall be implemented to describe how sensitive any outcome variable (for this proposal, the NPV in each scenario) to variations of input parameters. Since there are usually several input parameters, such technique can help in determining which parameter drives the majority of the deviations in the outcome [27].

Sensitivity analysis is commonly used in energy efficiency evaluations. For instance, Dae-HyunChoi and Le Xie (2016) recommend a novel analytical framework to measure the sensitivity of home energy management systems (HEMS) to fluctuations in input data for HEMS operation [28].

3. Statistical analysis

3.1 Methodology

In order to investigate different aspects of the study, several data collection methods were used such as questionnaire, interviews (site visits), and published data (through secondary research). The questionnaire targeted the end users, while the interviews targeted some major stakeholders in the air conditioning industry. The majority of the data analyzed in this chapter is coming from the questionnaire.

3.2 Questionnaire

3.2.1 Structure

The questionnaire had a total of 13 questions with the majority being of multiple-choice type which made it easier for respondents to respond and easier for the researcher to analyze. The survey was developed in Arabic using Google Docs platform.

3.2.2 Sample size

As per the Saudi General Authority of Statistics, the 2017 population of Saudi Arabia is around 20.4 million that the sample was drawn from. A statistically representative sample, using 99% confidence level and +/−5% confidence interval, would be less than 700 respondents (i.e., 666) using Survey System methodology as described in the below Equations [29]. The number of respondents in the study exceeded 4000, which is more than six times the needed sample size. The following formulas were used to calculate the needed sample size:

$$SS = \frac{Z^2 * (p) * (1 - p)}{C^2} \tag{4}$$

where SS is the sample size, Z is the Z value (2.58 for 99% confidence level), p is the percentage picking a choice, expressed as decimal (0.5 used for sample size needed), and C is the confidence interval, expressed as decimal ($0.05 = \pm 5$).

The sample size then needs to be corrected for a finite population as follows:

$$\text{New SS} = \frac{SS}{1 + \frac{SS - 1}{pop}} \tag{5}$$

where pop is the population (i.e., 20.4 million).

3.2.3 Results

The survey was run over a 1-week period. Over that period, the survey link received more than 7500 clicks. While the total number of responses exceeded 4700, only 4649 were included in the analysis as some of the answers were inconsistent and hence excluded. The response rate could not be determined exactly given the lack of statistics on who really saw the tweet, post, or message. The response-to-click ratio, yet, is around 63%.

The below figures show the sociodemographic profiles of the 4649 respondents used in the analysis. The following subgroup contains the majority of respondents in their respective sociodemographic categories: Income level, 9000–15,000 SR income group (36%); citizenship, Saudi (99.5%); marital status, married (82.4%); and age: 30–39 years age group (52.2%). Geographically, the highest representative administrated areas (regions) were central (49%), western (25%), and then eastern (15%).

It was noticed that some groups (Saudis, male, married, 30–39 years old) are over represented in the sample. This is not surprising given the fact that those groups are the ones who are interested in the topic at hand, which is good for the survey and its results.

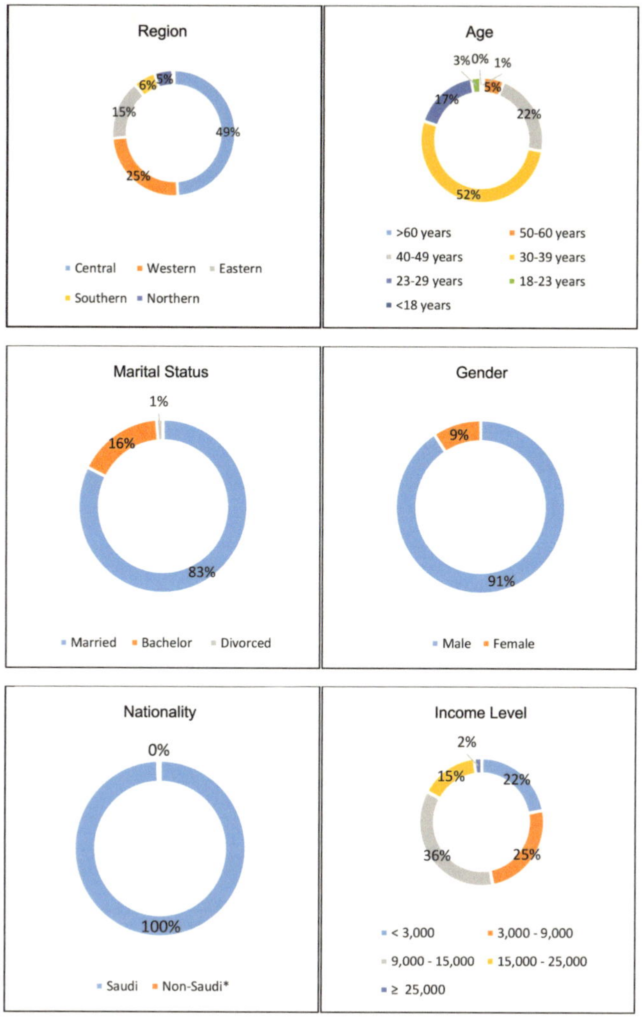

4. Program design

Before going into the details of the Residential Air Conditioning Incentive Program, below are the major assumptions undertaken during the development of the incentive program:

1. Administration cost of the program is not considered.

2. Units to be replaced are 10 years old or more. Moreover, old units are surrendered to program administrator when receiving the new unit.

3. Weighted average tonnage of the AC units is 2.0176 TR based on Saudi Label & Standard (SL&S) registration system.

4. Average annual operating hours is 2741.

5. 2016 existing residential stock of small units is around 23 million units.

6. Being conservative by assuming that old units to be replaced have EERs matching 2013 standard (i.e., window 7 and 8.5 for split).

7. Being conservative by not degrading the old units with temperature and only degrading the new units with temperature.

8. Benefits of installed ACs assumed to last for 20 years.

4.1 Program summary

Covered units	Ten-year-old or more residential window and split air conditioning units
Amount replaced	5.75 million units (i.e., 25% of 2016 stock) Window: 3.45 million unit Split: 2.3 million unit
Program duration	8 years
Program start/end years	Start on 2018 all the way to 2025
Replaced units' EER	Window: 7 Split: 8.5
New units' EER	Match exactly compliance standards at each specific year until 2022 where EERs of new units are fixed at that level until the year where the program ends (2025)

Based on the survey, by the time the program gets into the implementation phase, more than 33% of the ACs in the market would be 10 years old or more. The proposal is to replace 25% of 2016 stock as detailed in the below table.

Type	2018	2019	2020	2021	2022	2023	2024	2025	Total
Window	431,250	431,250	431,250	431,250	431,250	431,250	431,250	431,250	3,450,000
Split	287,500	287,500	287,500	287,500	287,500	287,500	287,500	287,500	2,300,000
Total	718,750	718,750	718,750	718,750	718,750	718,750	718,750	718,750	**5,750,000**

4.2 Stock estimates

The 2016 estimated stock of small units is composed of around 60 and 40% share of windows and split units, respectively. These shares are evolving over time as split units are becoming more favored by Saudi residential consumers, and hence the future percentage of shares are expected to shift more toward the split units in lieu of window units.

4.3 Costs

As in every incentive program, this program is capital-intensive. The main chunk of the capital is needed for the new air conditioning units that shall be installed. Moreover and in an effort to perform a sanity check of our utilized cost estimates, numbers were cross-checked through site visits to several retailers in Al-Khobar city where the average window unit price was around $384, whereas the price was $870 for split units which are not far away from our initial estimates. When discussing costs, our cost information may not address the expected increase in standards and their effects and only considered inflation along with normal technology evolution. In addition, a meeting with Zamil Air conditioners (the largest HVAC manufacturer in the Middle East) was held to check the impact of standards on the price of the units, and the below tables summarize the price impact on both manufacturers and end users.

- Impact on manufacturers

AC type	Increase in price (%) after the first increase in efficiency target	Increase in price (%) after the second increase in efficiency target
Window	7	10
Split	10	20

- Impact on end users

AC type	Increase in price (%) after the first increase in efficiency target	Increase in price (%) after the second increase in efficiency target
Window	5	10
Split	10	18

4.4 Energy efficiency ratio assumptions

By using compliance standard EER values at each specific year along with expected EER values at T1 in future years and utilizing the shares of the weighted average tonnage of small air conditioning units, it was found that the aggregated EER at T1 are as shown below:

EERs (T1)	2018	2019	2020	2021	2022	2023	2024	2025
Window	10.4	10.6	11.3	11.5	11.8	12	12.2	12.8
Split	12.6	12.8	13.9	14.2	14.5	14.8	15.1	15.5

In order to be conservative and not exaggerate with energy savings estimates, EER values beyond year 2022 were fixed at year 2022 levels. Hence, the aggregated EER values became as follows:

EERs (T1)	2018	2019	2020	2021	2022	2023	2024	2025
Window	10.4	10.6	11.3	11.5	11.8	11.8	11.8	11.8
Split	12.6	12.8	13.9	14.2	14.5	14.5	14.5	14.5

However, EER values are specified at T1 levels (i.e., 35 degree Celsius) only. It is known that the outside air temperature varies from 18 degrees Celsius where cooling load is required until extreme temperature levels which could occasionally exceed T3 levels of 46 degree Celsius. For the sake of this study, the analysis will be capped at T3 levels as beyond T3 levels are rarely reached. As an example, the average 15 years bin weather data for Dhahran City shows that only .58 of a day in the year is exceeding the 46 degree Celsius. This can be translated to only less than 0.2% of the years above the T3 level in Dhahran.

Although manufacturers provide EER values of an AC unit at several different outside air temperatures (OATs) including T1 (i.e., 35°C) and T3 (i.e., 46°C), they do not provide the EER value at each and every temperature above T1. Therefore, the EER value for each temperature point above T1 level needs to be identified first in order to be able to calculate the EER's percent reduction at each temperature value above T1. Hence, a linear regression model was applied for different Al-Zamil air conditioning window and split units with diverse EER values at T1. Then, the calculated weighted average value was utilized in energy savings calculations. The regression analysis was following the below equation:

$$Y = a + X \times b \tag{6}$$

where Y is the dependent variable (energy efficiency ratio of the air conditioner), X is the independent variable (outside air temperature), b is the slope of the line, and a is the y-intercept.

After performing the calculations on the different models, it was found that the weighted average EER drop for a given temperature above T1 value is around 2.1% per degree temperature. Thus, new window units' EER values (adjusted by taking into account EER degradation factor) were computed as follows:

Window								
Year	**2018**	**2019**	**2020**	**2021**	**2022**	**2023**	**2024**	**2025**
Adjusted EER	9.66	9.85	10.51	10.72	10.94	10.94	10.94	10.94

Similarly, new split units' EER values (adjusted by taking into account EER degradation factor) were calculated as follows:

Split								
Year	**2018**	**2019**	**2020**	**2021**	**2022**	**2023**	**2024**	**2025**
Adjusted EER	11.7	11.93	12.94	13.2	13.46	13.46	13.46	13.46

Having said that, the units subject to replacement (10 years old or more) are assumed to have the below EER values at T1. In order to be conservative with the calculation, T1 values for old units are used in calculating the corresponding energy consumption without considering the degradation with temperature:

EER at T1 for units subject to replacement										
Year	**2016**	**2017**	**2018**	**2019**	**2020**	**2021**	**2022**	**2023**	**2024**	**2025**
Window	7	7	7	7	7	7	7	7	7	7
Split	8.5	8.5	8.5	8.5	8.5	8.5	8.5	8.5	8.5	8.5

5. Results and discussion

In this section of the chapter, energy savings resulting from the replacement of existing air conditioning units with new ones will be presented along with the economic impact from NPV, gross domestic product, and employment perspectives. The presented results will be also discussed in details in this section.

5.1 Energy savings

In order to quantify the overall savings of the program, the calculation started with quantifying the saved energy per unit going from a low-level EER to the proposed level at each specific year. Then, the saved energy per unit was multiplied by the replaced stock at that year in order to get the overall yearly savings. This approach was applied for both window and split units as can be comprehended from the below equations and tables:

$$EER = \frac{\text{Desired Output}\left(\text{i.e.cooling load in}\frac{\text{BTU}}{\text{h}}\right)}{\text{Required Input (i.e.electri power in W)}} \tag{7}$$

Knowing that 1 TR equals 12,000 BTU/h and the weighted average tonnage (TR) of the AC units is 2.0176,

$$\text{Annual KWh of Air Conditioner} = \frac{12 \times \text{TR} \times \text{Average Annual Operating Hours}}{\text{EER}} \tag{8}$$

- *Window*

Year	New EER	Existing EER	New unit's Kwh	Existing unit's Kwh	Savings per unit	No. of units	Savings (TWh)
2018	9.66	7	6870	9480	2611	431,250	1.13
2019	9.85	7	6736	9480	2745	431,250	1.18
2020	10.51	7	6315	9480	3165	431,250	1.37
2021	10.72	7	6189	9480	3291	431,250	1.42
2022	10.94	7	6068	9480	3412	431,250	1.47
2023	10.94	7	6068	9480	3412	431,250	1.47
2024	10.94	7	6068	9480	3412	431,250	1.47
2025	10.94	7	6068	9480	3412	431,250	1.47

- *Split*

Year	New EER	Existing EER	New unit's Kwh	Existing unit's Kwh	Savings per unit	No. of units	Savings (TWh)
2018	11.70	8.5	5673	7807	2134	287,500	0.61
2019	11.93	8.5	5562	7807	2245	287,500	0.65
2020	12.94	8.5	5130	7807	2677	287,500	0.77
2021	13.20	8.5	5029	7807	2778	287,500	0.8
2022	13.46	8.5	4932	7807	2875	287,500	0.83
2023	13.46	8.5	4932	7807	2875	287,500	0.83
2024	13.46	8.5	4932	7807	2875	287,500	0.83
2025	13.46	8.5	4932	7807	2875	287,500	0.83

As can be seen from the above tables, the energy savings from window units starts at 1.13 TWh in the first year of the program and reaches 1.47 TWh on year 2022 onward. Similarly for split units, the savings starts from 0.61 TWh in 2018 and level at 0.83 TWh on year 2022 onward. The savings are higher from window replacements mainly due to the fact that the number of replaced units is higher than those of split units on yearly basis.

The savings from window and split units are added together in order to get the overall yearly savings along with the cumulative savings.

Year	Savings in TWh from windows	Saving in TWh from splits	TWh (yearly)	TWh (cumulative)
2018	1.13	0.61	1.74	
2019	1.18	0.65	1.83	3.57
2020	1.37	0.77	2.13	5.7
2021	1.42	0.8	2.22	7.92
2022	1.47	0.83	2.3	10.22
2023	1.47	0.83	2.3	12.52
2024	1.47	0.83	2.3	14.82
2025	1.47	0.83	2.3	17.11

As per Electricity and Cogeneration Regulatory Authority (ECRA) open data, the kingdom consumed, in 2017, around 298 TWh of electricity, while 143 TWh of this consumption was in the residential sector alone [30]. Therefore, the cumulative savings from the program would represent 6% of the 2017 kingdom's total electricity consumption and 12% of the residential sector. Of course this percent would reduce over time as the consumption of the kingdom is expected to increase progressively mainly due to more electrification, population growth, and economic development, yet still the numbers are considerable. Moreover, this suggested program would result in a reduction of a yearly average 7.5 million metric ton of $CO2$ emissions which is basically equivalent to removing 1.38 million cars from the streets or planting more than 27 million trees.

Furthermore, and assuming 80% utilization rate, the cumulative saved energy of 17.11 TWh by 2025 is equivalent to a power plant with around 2.5 GW of capacity. This 2.5 GW represents around 3% of 2017 kingdom's total capacity. The proposed program will help basically in shaving peak loads, reducing energy growth rates in addition to the avoided capital.

It is worth mentioning that the minimum annual SAR savings per AC unit for residential customer varies from SAR 248 to 324 per window unit and from SAR 203 to 432 per split unit depending on EER levels between new and replaced units.

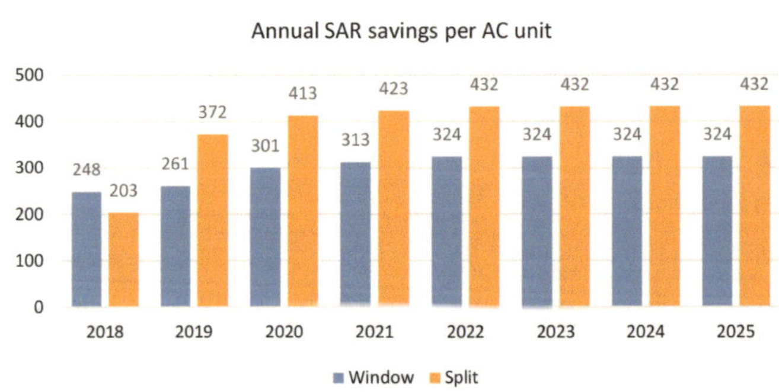

5.2 Economic analysis

5.2.1 Net present value (NPV) and sensitivity analysis

Using 5.3% as commercial discount rates over 20-year impact period of new equipment, the net present value (NPV) summaries are shown below for three different scenarios.

1. Assuming the government will take the burden of the full cost of the new units

Type	$ Billion
PV cost (i = 5.3%)	2.74
PV savings (i = 5.3%)	16.44
NPV (i = 5.3%)	13.7

2. Based on the online survey results, a weighted average of 25% of the cost can be absorbed by the households. Hence, the government will take care of only 75% of the cost, and the results will be as follows

Type	$ Billion
PV cost (i = 5.3%)	2.03
PV savings (i = 5.3%)	16.44
NPV (i = 5.3%)	14.40

3. The capital cost will be transferred solely to non-efficient equipment buyers. Hence, almost no contribution from the government

Type	$ Billion
PV cost (i = 5.3%)	0
PV savings (i = 5.3%)	16.44
NPV (i = 5.3%)	16.44

The third scenario basically uses the "feebate" system where the government transfers the whole cost to consumers, and hence the government will not bear the capital cost of the equipment. They will only need to pay for administration cost although even the administration cost can be transferred to consumers depending on the fee rates on non-efficient equipment.

In summary and as can be seen from the above tables, the NPVs in all the three scenarios are positive with great values, and hence proceeding with the program is vital for the Saudi government at this stage and with any of the above scenarios. Thorough assessment of those scenarios and others shall be performed prior to program deployment and the program administrator shall critically evaluate several factors including, but not limited to, current market situation, manufacturer willingness, retailer/distributer readiness, government funding availability, etc.

A sensitivity analysis has been applied to the NPVs of all the three scenarios to check how sensitive the results are to several selected input variables that have been applied across all the scenarios. Five input variables were selected for the sensitivity analysis, and they are air conditioner cost, assumed EER values of the existing air conditioner fleet, assumed EER values of the new air conditioner fleet, utility discount rate, and the average annual operating hours of air conditioners. The applied variabilities to the input variables were ± 25% for each variable. The below table summarizes the results of the analysis.

Input variables	**Scenario 1 (100% gov.)**		**Scenario 2 (75% gov.)**		**Scenario 3 (0% gov.)**	
	NPV ($ billion)	**% Difference**	**NPV ($b)**	**% Diff.**	**NPV ($b)**	**% Diff.**
AC unit cost (+25%)	13.2	3%	14	3%	16.4	0%
AC unit cost (−25%)	14.5	−7%	15	−4%	16.4	0%
Assumed EER values of existing fleet (+25%)	6.8	50%	7.5	48%	9.6	41%
Assumed EER values of existing fleet (−25%)	24.8	−82%	25.5	−77%	27.5	−68%
Assumed EER values of new fleet (+25%)	18.3	−35%	18.9	−31%	21	−28%
Assumed EER values of new fleet (−25%)	6	56%	6.8	53%	8.8	46%
Utility discount rate (+25%)	11.2	18%	11.9	17%	13.8	16%
Utility discount rate (−25%)	16.9	−24%	17.7	−23%	19.9	−21%
Average annual operating hours of AC unit (+25%)	16.6	−22%	17.3	−20%	19.3	−18%
Average annual operating hours of AC unit (−25%)	10.8	21%	11.5	20%	13.5	18%
Current proposal NPV ($ billion)	**13.6**		**14.4**		**16.4**	

It can be noticed that varying the EER values whether for the existing or new fleets has the biggest impact on the results, while the input variable with the least impact among the five is the air conditioner unit cost. It can be also noticed from the above table that the AC unit cost variable has no impact on scenario three results as in this scenario the capital cost is transferred to non-efficient air conditioner buyers with no contribution from the government. In summary, despite applying aggressive variabilities to key input variables in all the three scenarios, the results still show positive net present values for all the scenarios which indicate that this proposal is valid and also highly recommended for deployment in order to reap such huge benefits.

5.2.2 GDP and employment contribution

In addition to the savings expected to be realized out of implementing the incentive program, there are other economic gains. Using input–output analysis ("I-O"), it was found that the program will add an average of $0.5 billion per year to the kingdom's GDP for the duration of the program. It was also estimated that around 2000 direct and indirect jobs will be created throughout the duration of the program.

The input–output analysis ("I-O") used in the analysis is a form of economic analysis based on the interdependencies between economic sectors. This method is most commonly used for estimating the impacts of positive or negative economic shocks and analyzing the ripple effects throughout an economy.

6. Conclusion

This chapter investigated the savings from a residential air conditioning incentive program rather than detailing the design of the program as this needs specialized entities who should evaluate different factors before designing such program. The proposed 8-year program included residential air conditioning units, namely, window and split, where participants are provided with efficient AC units as a substitute to their existing low efficiency AC units. The program was designed to replace 5.75 million AC units (25% of estimated 2016 stock) over an 8-year period. The proposal was presented under three different scenarios when it comes to the capital cost handling where the government will take care of all the capital cost, 75%, and none of the capital cost in scenarios 1, 2, and 3, respectively. The cumulative estimated savings from the program adds up to 17.11 TWh by the year 2025. Moreover, this suggested program would result in a reduction of a yearly average of 7.5 million metric ton of CO2 emissions which is basically equivalent to removing 1.38 million cars from the streets or planting more than 27 million trees. Furthermore, the expected NPVs from the program are substantial, and they are $13.7 billion, $14.4 billion, and $16.4 billion under the three different scenarios. From the economics perspective, the program will add an average of $0.5 billion per year to the kingdom's GDP over the duration of the program. It was also estimated that around 2000 direct and indirect jobs will be created throughout the duration of the program.

As incentive programs regularly take care of the initial investment cost of energy-efficient products and hence implicate significant capitalization, the program administrator shall evaluate different experiences from developed and developing nations to instigate the development of new funding mechanisms to suit unique local circumstances such as Saudi Arabia. In addition, such programs will support the country's current efforts to improve the permeation of energy-efficient equipment in the Saudi market. Subsidy programs are essential to balance the present compulsory standards by increasing market permeation of equipment that have better energy performance than current standards requirement, therefore paving the road for further increase in standards stringency in the future. Moreover, the program administrator shall comprehend the fact that the success of such program depends heavily on an outstanding plan in place before the program initiation. The plans shall include monitoring and verification plans along with continuous evaluation plans in place in which a reserved budget for those purposes is crucial.

Acknowledgements

The author would like to extend sincere thanks to Hussien Mohammad, from Saudi Aramco, for his support in obtaining bin weather data for several Saudi cities along with his support in reviewing the EER degradation analysis. Also, the author would like to thank Aabed Saber, from Saudi Aramco, for his contribution in reviewing the chapter and providing useful insights especially concerning the questionnaire.

Author details

Faisal Fahad Al-Musa
Saudi Aramco, Dhahran, Saudi Arabia

*Address all correspondence to: faisal.mousa.1@aramco.com

References

[1] de la Rue du Can S et al. Design of incentive programs for accelerating penetration of energy-efficient appliances. Energy Policy. 2014;**72**: 56-66

[2] Sathaye J, Murtishaw S. Market Failures, Consumer Preferences, and Transaction Costs in Energy Efficiency Purchase Decisions. CA, USA: Public Interest Energy Research (PIER) Program; 2004

[3] Jollands N, Waide P, Ellis M, Onoda T, Laustsen J, Tanaka K, et al. The 25 IEA energy efficiency policy recommendations to the G8 Gleneagles plan of action. Energy Policy. 2010; **38**(11):6409-6418

[4] Murphy L, Meier F. Waking a sleeping Giant: Policy tools to improve the energy performance of the existing housing stock in the Netherlands. In: European Council for Energy-Efficient Economy, Summer Study. France: La Colle Sur Loup. 2011. p. 2011

[5] Hausman J. Individual discount rates and the purchase and utilization of energy-using durables. Bell Journal of Economics. 1979;**10**:33-54

[6] Houston DA. Implicit discount rates and the purchase of untried, energy-saving durable goods. Journal of Consumer Research. 1983;**10**:236-246

[7] Independent Pricing and Regulatory Tribunal (IPART). Compliance and Operation of the NSW Energy Savings Scheme During 2009. Report to Minister, New South Wales; 2010

[8] Balawant J. Best Practices in Designing and Implementing Energy Efficiency Obligation Schemes. Research Report Task XXII of the International Energy Agency Demand Side Management Programme; 2012

[9] Lees E. Energy Efficiency Obligations —The EU Experience. European Council for an Energy Efficient Economy, Briefing for DG Energy on EU Energy Efficiency Obligations on Energy Companies and Their Importance in Meeting Climate Change and Energy Security Challenges; 2012

[10] Taylor RP, Govindarajalu C, Levin J, Meyer A, Ward W. Financing Energy Efficiency: Lessons from Brazil, China, India, and Beyond. Washington, DC: World Bank and International Bank for Reconstruction and Development (IBRD); 2008

[11] Sathaye J, de la Rue du Can S, Kumar S, Iyer M, Galitsky C, Phadke A, et al. Implementing End-use Efficiency Improvements in India: Drawing from Experience in the US and Other Countries. Lawrence Berkeley National Laboratory report LBNL—60035; 2006

[12] Chunekar A, Singh D. A Guide Book on Super-Efficient Equipment Program (SEEP). Pune, India: Prayas Energy Group. 2013

[13] International Energy Agency (IEA). Energy Efficiency Governance; 2010. Available from: www.iea.org/papers/2010/eeg.pdf

[14] Rosenberg M, Hoefgen L. Market Effects and Market Transformation: Their Role in Energy Efficiency Program Design and Evaluation. California Institute for Energy and Environment; 2009. Available from: http://uc-ciee.org/downloads/mrkt_effts_wp.pdf

[15] Eto J, Goldman C, Nadel S. Ratepayer-Funded Energy-Efficiency Programs in a Restructured Electricity Industry: Issues and Options for Regulators and Legislators. Lawrence Berkeley National Laboratory Report LBNL-41479; 1998

[16] Rogers EM. Diffusion of Innovations. 5th ed. New York: Free Press; 2003

[17] Gold R, Nadel S. Energy Efficiency Tax Incentive, 2005–2011: How Have They Performed? American Council for an Energy Efficient Economy White Paper; 2011. Available from: http://aceee.org/files/pdf/white-paper/Tax%20incentive%20white%20paper.pdf

[18] U. S. Environmental Protection Agency (U.S.EPA). Aligning utility incentives with investment in energy efficiency. National action plan for energy efficiency, prepared by Val R. Jensen. ICF Int. 2007. Available from: www.epa.gov/eeactionplan

[19] French Ministry of Sustainable Development. Le Point sur le Crédit D'impôt Déve- loppement Durable. Commissariat General au Developpement Durable, Le Point sur—Numéro147–Octobre. 2012. Available from: http://www.territoires.gouv.fr/IMG/pdf/LPS147.pdf

[20] Pistochini P, Valentini G. The 55% tax reductions for building retrofitting in Italy: The results. In: EEDAL 2011 International Conference. 2011

[21] Salaverría A, Patricia D. Evaluación Ambiental y Plan de Mane jo Ambiental del Programa de Eficiencia Energética Coordinado por la Secretaría de Energía: Informe Final. SENER. KfW Group, World Bank; 2010

[22] Scott D. The energy system. The International Journal of Hydrogen Energy. 1994;**19**:485-490

[23] Al-Musa F, Youssef A, Yassein M. Potential energy savings by switching residential cooking and water heating appliances from electric to LPG in Saudi Arabia. In: ASHRAE Winter Conference. 2016

[24] McNeil Michael, Iyer Maithili, Meyers Stephen, Letschert Virginie, McMahon James E. Potential Benefits from Improved Energy Efficiency of Key Electrical Products: The Case of India. Environmental Energy Technologies Division, Lawrence Berkeley National Laboratory, University of California; 2005

[25] Taner T. Optimisation processes of energy efficiency for a drying plant: A case of study for Turkey. Applied Thermal Engineering. 2015;**80**:247-260

[26] Muller DCA, Marechal FMA, Wolewinski T, Roux PJ. An energy management method for the food industry. Applied Thermal Engineering. 2007;**27**:2677-2688

[27] Lauer M. Methodology guideline on techno economic assessment (TEA). Generated in the framework of ThermalNet WP3B economics. In: Thermal Net TEA Methodology Guideline. 2008

[28] Choi D-H, Xie L. A framework for sensitivity analysis of data errors on home energy management system. Energy. 2016;**117**:166-175

[29] Available from: https://www.surveysystem.com/sample-size-formula.htm

[30] Available from: http://www.ecra.gov.sa/enus/DataAndStatistics/NationalRecord/HistoricalData/Pages/Home.aspx

Chapter 4

Primary Energy Factor for Electricity Mix: The Case of Slovenia

Matjaž Prek

Abstract

According to the European energy policy, the energy use of technical systems in buildings is given at the level of primary energy. This calculation requires knowledge of the primary energy conversion factors according to their source; however, there is currently no single European-wide recognized method for their determination. The aim of this study is to present and compare three methods for determining primary energy factors, namely the method of partial substitution, the physical energy method, and calculation according to EN 15603 standard. For the case study, the electricity factor for Slovenia was calculated according to the aforementioned methods. The results of this study showed that the methods differ in the evaluation of individual primary sources, which has a significant impact on the PEF value. We found that with the partial substitution method, we do not get representative results about the PEF. The method of physical energy defines the efficiency of production from renewable energy sources as 100%. The question arises if we can truly assume that the use of PE is equal to the actual production of electricity. In the third method, defined in the EN 15603 standard, which provides two PEFs, a certain measure of criticality of the assumed factors for the different sources of energy is used.

Keywords: primary energy, primary energy factor, electricity mix, renewable energy sources

1. Introduction

The building sector in Europe is responsible for 40% of energy consumption and 36% of CO_2 emissions. Due to the high estimated energy saving potential of the building sector, the European Union (EU) set up a policy framework focused on reducing the energy of buildings which consists of policy actions, i.e., Energy Performance of Buildings Directive (EPBD) [1], Energy Efficiency Directive (EED) [2], EcoDesign Directive [3], Energy Labelling Regulation [4], and the Renewable Energy Directive (RED) [5]. The EED was prepared with the goal to achieve a 20% energy consumption reduction target across the EU. It establishes a number of important provisions to be implemented by the EU Member States, including the requirement to establish obligatory national energy efficiency targets, national building energy efficiency strategies, a requirement to renovate 3% of public sector buildings annually, the need to establish energy efficiency obligation schemes, and provisions for auditing and metering.

The evaluation of energy consumption, reduction, or efficiency on the building level is somehow problematic since different technical systems use various forms of energy to operate. Therefore, energy consumption and efficiency should be evaluated on a common basis. A single metric for combining different sources or types of energy is primary energy (PE). As the name indicates, PE evaluates different forms of energy based on the conversion of primary energy to useful energy. However, the concept does not differentiate between different energy forms. Therefore, exergy could be incorporated into the concept as it reflects the energy "quality" in terms of its capacity to do work. Although there are currently no requests, for such an approach, from energy practitioners, exergy analysis could gain significantly on importance in light of future resource scarcity to, for example, penalize the use of exergy-rich energy vectors for low-temperature applications.

The task of measuring energy efficiency may seem straightforward, contingent only on the choice of indicators for the input and output. In reality, however, both can be measured in numerous ways, and choosing one approach over another always leads to trade-offs [6–11]. Based on the input and output characteristics, three main indicator groups can be distinguished:

- Thermodynamic indicators—inputs and outputs represented in terms of thermodynamic quantities (e.g., the thermal efficiency of a heating system)
- Physical-thermodynamic indicators—energy inputs represented by thermodynamic quantities, outputs represented with physical units (e.g., building energy use intensity)
- Economic-thermodynamic indicators—products or services represented by market prices, energy represented by means of thermodynamic quantities (e.g., GDP energy intensity)

Each of these approaches has its advantages and disadvantages and should, thus, be defined with regard to the area of application, while considering environmental, social, economic, or other aspects of energy efficiency.

PE has become an important policy metric in the EU. Namely, the EPBD prescribes that the energy performance of a building shall also include a numeric indicator of PE, based on primary energy factors (PEF) per energy carrier, which may be based on national or regional annual weighted averages or a specific value for onsite production. A PEF connects primary and final energy. It indicates how much primary energy is used to generate a unit of electricity or a unit of useable thermal energy. The PEF describes the efficiency of converting energy from primary sources (e.g., coal, crude oil) to a secondary energy carrier (e.g., electricity, natural gas) that provides energy services delivered to end users. In the EU, the Member States can freely define its value. Consequently, this has become a political decision, with a direct impact on the actual energy consumption of a building.

Similar concept of analysis of the impact of building and appliance energy consumption is used in the USA. Compared to the more legislative-constrained EU approach the US approach is more market oriented. Full-fuel-cycle (FFC) metrics are used in building codes and appliance standards to evaluate the energy and environmental impact of consumer fuels and appliances [12].

To translate PE into final energy use, the PEF is applied in several EU legislative documents. In the EED and EPBD, the PEF is used to convert final energy consumption into PE consumption to monitor progress against targets. The EPB Directive aims at reducing the PE demand for buildings. Since technologies applied in the building and improvements in the building envelope lead to savings in final energy, the PEF is applied to convert these savings into primary energy.

The latest version of the EPB Directive [13] claims that "the energy performance of a building shall be expressed by a numeric indicator of PE use for the purpose of both energy performance certification and compliance with minimum energy performance requirements." In addition, Member States may define additional numeric indicators of total nonrenewable and renewable primary energy use and of greenhouse gas emission. Member States have some flexibility in defining these metrics.

EED requires energy targets expressed in both primary and final energy form. PEFs are applied for conversion of final energy savings into primary energy savings. EPBD and EED both allow the Member States the option of choosing their own PEF values. Within the EcoDesign Directive and Energy Labelling Directive, the PEF value of 2.5 for electricity is prescribed to allow a comparison.

From the foregoing, it is evident that the PEF is defined on two different boundary conditions within the EU legislation. For instance, the boundary condition for energy-consuming appliances is defined at the appliance level. The next level of boundary is the building (or part of it), defined as a sum of all energy used by different appliances considering different energy sources. This boundary condition is important when on-site-produced renewable energy is used by building appliances.

The method for calculating the PE for fossil fuels is quite straightforward and consistent, while the calculation of PEFs for electricity or heat generated from renewable energies or grid-supplied electricity is more complex. First of all, the PEF for fossil fuels (also for combustible renewable fuels) does not change significantly over time. For electricity, especially grid supplied, the calculation of PEF involves different energy sources as well as different electricity generation technologies. The combination of various PE sources forms a so-called power generation mix, which is the share of different energy sources used to generate electricity. The share of energy sources changes over time depending on the availability of energy sources and the level of demand. However, evaluating this is a challenge especially in renewable energy sources and nuclear energy.

2. Methodology

PE sources are usually defined as inputs into energy systems (or conversion processes) which convert them into secondary energy carriers such as electricity, oil products, heat, or mechanical work. The EPBD [13] defines primary energy as the energy that has not been subjected to any (human induced) conversion or transformation process.

As mentioned before, PEF connects primary and final energy. It indicates how much primary energy is used to generate a unit of electricity or a unit of useable thermal energy, according to Eq. (1):

$$PEF = \frac{primary\ energy}{final\ energy} \tag{1}$$

PE is divided into renewable and nonrenewable energy [14]. The sum of renewable and nonrenewable energy is total energy. Energy extracted from sources that are naturally replenished on a human timescale is called renewable energy. The definition of renewable energy also includes some forms of energy carrier such as biomass and energy recovered from waste. For nonrenewable energy sources, the extraction rate is higher than refill rate. Energy obtained from nonrenewable energy sources is called nonrenewable energy. This approach enables the determination of three primary energy factors for each energy carrier [14, 15]:

- Total primary energy factor (PEF_{tot}) (Eq. (2))
- Nonrenewable primary energy factor (PEF_{nren}) (Eq. (3))
- Renewable primary energy factor (PEF_{ren}) (Eq. (4))

$$PEF_{tot} = \frac{total\ \ primary\ \ energy}{delivered\ \ non-renewable + delivered\ \ renewable\ \ energy} \tag{2}$$

$$PEF_{nren} = \frac{non-renewable\ \ primary\ \ energy}{delivered\ \ non-renewable + delivered\ \ renewable\ \ energy} \tag{3}$$

$$PEF_{ren} = \frac{renewable\ \ primary\ \ energy}{delivered\ \ non-renewable + delivered\ \ renewable\ \ energy} \tag{4}$$

Energy sources can be further divided into combustible and noncombustible. Where primary energy is used to characterize fossil fuels, the embodied energy of the fuel is available as thermal energy, and typically around 70% is lost in conversion to electrical or mechanical energy.

In accordance with the laws of thermodynamics, the renewable PEF can be derived from the relevant energy conversion efficiency. For example, the electricity from a PV system with an overall efficiency of 20% can be considered to have a renewable PEF of 5. There is a similar 60–80% conversion loss when wind energy is converted to electricity. This also applies to nuclear energy, where only around 10% of the fuel's energy content is converted to electricity.

Although primary energy factors are thermodynamically universal, many different calculation methods exist. Moreover, there are also national variations. In order to calculate the PEFs, two approaches are mainly used, namely the partial substitution method and the physical energy method. They differ in the way how to calculate the PEFs from nuclear power plants and renewable energy sources such as hydroelectric power plants, solar energy, geothermal energy, etc.

The partial substitution method solves the aforementioned problem by concentrating on the theoretical energy content in traditional fossil fuels (coal, oil, and gas). The PEF for a mixture of electricity is calculated from these sources by dividing the energy content of the fuel as the input energy with the generated electricity. In the case of renewable energy and nuclear energy, this means calculating how much primary energy would be needed for such an amount of electricity if it were produced from fossil fuels.

The physical energy method differs from the partial substitution method in that it uses a different approach for the evaluation of primary energy in the production of electricity from hydro, wind, and nuclear power plants. The calculation of the PEF for the production of electricity from nuclear and geothermal energy is based on the thermal energy of the steam boiler that drives the turbine of the power plant. The efficiency of nuclear power plants is estimated at 33 and 10% for geothermal. For other renewable energy sources, such as hydro, wind, and solar energy, this is equal to gross electricity production.

The calculation of the PEF can also be made using the method described in the standard SIST EN 15603:2008 [15]. The standard describes two alternative approaches for calculating the factor, namely, the total and nonrenewable PEF. The difference between these factors is that the latter does not include the use of renewable energy. In addition, the national PEF for the electricity mix is based either on the average electricity mix or on the marginal electricity production. The standard defines the default PEFs for different energy sources, including electricity. The values of the factors are given in **Table 1**.

We made a calculation of the PEF for the electricity mix in Slovenia, based on the three previously described methods, and conducted a temporal comparison. Statistical data on the generation of electricity from individual sources were obtained from the Statistical Office of Slovenia [16]. **Table 2** shows the produced electricity by years from various sources of energy.

The electricity mix in Slovenia is mainly composed of five sources of primary energy, namely nuclear, fossil, hydro, wind, and solar energy. Since Slovenia is a member of the EU, the directives stipulate that, by 2020, as much as 20% of the energy used is to be recovered from renewable energy sources as far as electricity is concerned. Therefore, in addition to calculating the factor for previous years, we have also tried to predict the generation of energy from individual sources, using linear regression, and then determine the resulting PEF for the electricity mix and the share of renewable sources. **Figure 1** presents the sources of energy, the share of energy sources in the production of electricity, and the share of energy from renewable sources.

Figure 1 shows that electricity generation from fossil fuels is somewhat lower, while production from solar energy and hydro resources is increasing. Generally speaking, the share of renewable resources is increasing. Wind energy represents a very small share; therefore, increasing the share is not noticeable from the figure, but if we look at **Table 1**, we see that production is slowly increasing from 2013 onward.

2.1 Calculation of primary energy factor by partial substitution method

In this method, the PE equivalent of the sources of electricity generation represents the amount of energy that would be necessary to generate an identical amount of electricity with conventional thermal power plants [17]. The PE equivalent is calculated using an average generating efficiency of these plants. This method has several shortcomings including the difficulty of choosing an appropriate energy conversion efficiency to determine the energy value of renewable energy

	PEF	
	Nonrenewable	**Total**
Fuel oil	1.35	1.35
Gas	1.36	1.36
Biomass	0.07	1.07
Hydro power plant (electricity)	0.5	1.5
Nuclear power plant (electricity)	2.8	2.8
Coal power plant (electricity)	4.05	4.05

Table 1.
Primary energy factors according to the Standard EN 15603:2008.

	Year															
	2002	**2003**	**2004**	**2005**	**2006**	**2007**	**2008**	**2009**	**2010**	**2011**	**2012**	**2013**	**2014**	**2015**	**2016**	**2017**
Nuclear	5528	5207	5459	5884	5548	5695	6273	5739	5657	6215	5528	5300	6370	5648	5715	6285
Fossil	5759	5657	5718	5772	5975	6082	6107	5945	6067	6073	5958	5661	4440	5081	5718	5610
Hydro	3313	2957	4095	3461	3591	3266	4018	4715	4703	3706	4087	4923	6366	4091	4782	4141
Wind	0	0	0	0	0	0	0	0	0	0	0	4	4	6	6	6
Solar	0	0	0	0	0	0	1	4	13	66	163	215	257	274	267	283

Table 2.
Yearly historical data on the electricity production in Slovenia (values in GWh) [16].

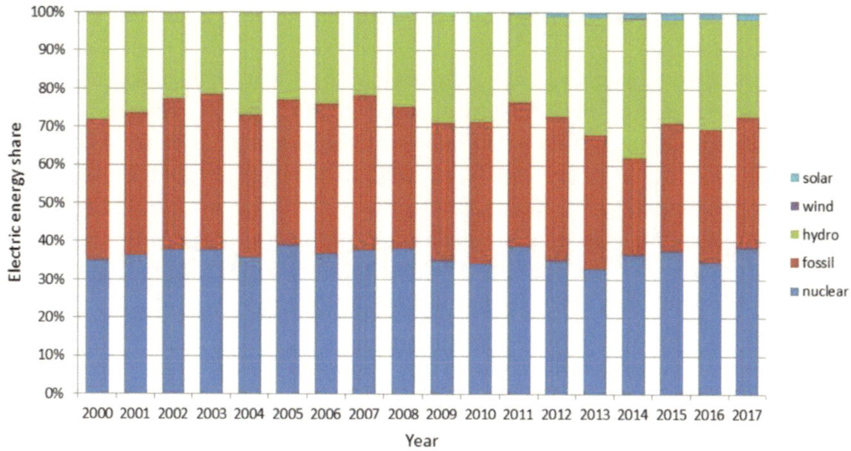

Figure 1.
Electricity mix in Slovenia.

and nuclear energy. For example, it may not be possible to quantify the energy content in the wind or the sun that serves as a fuel for wind and solar power plants. In conventional nuclear power plants, only 10% of the theoretical energy content in the fuel is converted to electricity. The partial substitution solves this challenge by focusing on the theoretical energy content of traditional fossil fuels (coal, gas, and oil). PEF for electricity produced from these sources is calculated by dividing the energy content of the fuel with the electricity production. For renewable and nuclear power, the partial substitution method calculates how much PE would be required if the electricity was generated from fossil fuels. Therefore, a conversion efficiency of 40% is assumed for these types of energy [18]. Also the efficiency of fossil fuel production is 40%. By means of these set values, we obtained for 2017 the results shown in **Table 3**.

As mentioned above, PE was obtained by dividing the energy produced by the production efficiency. This gave us the amount of PE needed to produce a certain amount of electricity. PE does not take into account the network losses; therefore, we calculated how much the losses are and what is our consumption. From this data we could then directly calculate the PEF for the electricity mix. We assumed that the amount of losses was 10% of the energy produced [18]. If by this method the factors are calculated for all the years, we can see that the factors do not change, which is because we have assumed that the efficiency is always the same, so the ratio between the energy used and the electricity produced is constant.

	Production [GWh]	Efficiency	Primary energy [GWh]
Nuclear	6285	40%	14,288
Fossil	5610	40%	14,295
Hydro	4141	40%	11,955
Wind	6	40%	15
Solar	283	40%	668
Total	16,325		40,813

Table 3.
Calculation of PE by partial substitution method for the production of electricity in Slovenia in 2017.

2.2 Calculation of primary energy factor by physical energy content method

The energy content method distinguishes itself in the approach for evaluating renewable sources and nuclear power plants production [19, 20]. PE in this method is considered as the first practically utilizable energy flow. In the case of directly combustible energy carriers (e.g., coal, natural gas, oil, biogas, bio liquids, solid biomass, combustible municipal/industrial waste), PE is defined as the heat generated in the combustion process. For non-directly combustible energy sources, PE can be expressed with the produced heat (e.g., nuclear, geothermal and solar thermal) or produced electricity (e.g., solar photovoltaic, wind, hydro, tide, wave, and ocean).

A PEF value of 1 is assumed for fuels. For noncombustible renewables a conversion efficiency of 100% is assumed. In contrast, a conversion efficiency of 33% is assumed for nuclear power stations. For combustible renewables such as biomass, the conversion efficiency is calculated from [15]. The resulting PEF for electricity from the various sources are 1 for hydro, wind, and solar PV; 3–4 for biomass; and 3 for solar thermal and nuclear. The results for 2017 are shown in **Table 4**.

Just like at the partial substitution method, we took into account 10% losses in the network to obtain the PE shown in **Table 5**.

The calculated PEF for the electricity mix using the physical energy method for 2017 is 2.55. For this year, this value is similar to the value assumed for Slovenia, i.e., 2.5. In order to observe the temporal variation of PEF, the same calculations were also carried out for previous years, based on statistical data for Slovenia. The results are illustrated in **Figure 2**.

Figure 2 shows that the factor is constantly changing, but we can notice that from 2011 onward the factor has fallen slightly. The likely reason for this is that the share of renewable resources began to increase markedly in the meantime. Since this method assumes 100% conversion efficiency for electricity produced from renewable sources, the primary energy for production is the same as production itself.

2.3 Calculation of the primary energy factor according to the Standard EN 15603:2008

The last calculation was carried out by using the default PEFs prescribed by the standard SIST EN 15603 [15]. This methodology evaluates separately the nonrenewable part and the total part of PE. Solar energy (PV) was evaluated in the same way as water and wind energy. Therefore, the default factors are the same in this case. In this method, we used the fractions of individual energies which comprise the mixture of electricity from **Table 1**. The full calculation for 2017 is shown in **Table 6**.

	Production [GWh]	Efficiency	Primary energy [GWh]
Nuclear	6285	33%	19,045
Fossil	5610	40%	14,025
Hydro	4141	100%	4141
Wind	6	100%	6
Solar (PV)	283	100%	283
Total	16,325		37,500

Table 4.
Calculation of PE by physical energy content method for the electricity production in Slovenia in 2017.

	Production [GWh]	Network loss [GWh]	Useful energy [GWh]	Primary energy [GWh]	PEF
Total	16,325	1632.5	14,692	37,500	2.55

Table 5.
Calculation of PEF by physical energy content method for the electricity production in Slovenia in 2017.

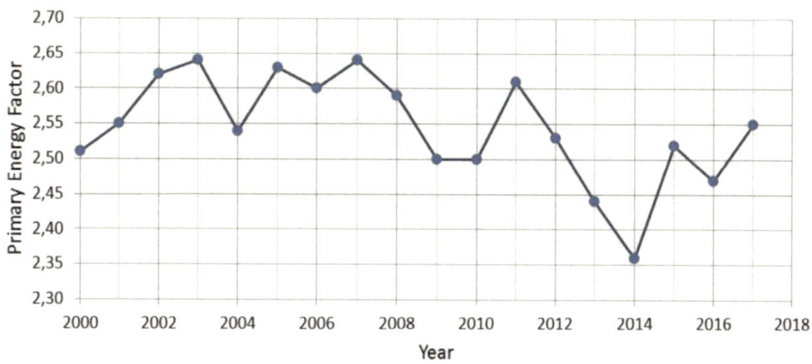

Figure 2.
PEFs for the electricity mix in Slovenia using the physical energy method for the years 2000–2018.

2017	PEF [/]				
	Nonrenewable	Total	Slovenia (average)		
			Energy share [%]	Nonrenewable	Total
Nuclear	2.8	2.8	38.5	1.05	1.08
Fossil	4.05	4.05	34.36	1.39	1.39
Hydro	0.5	1.5	25.37	0.13	0.38
Wind	0.5	1.5	0.04	0.00	0.00
Solar	0.5	1.5	1.73	0.01	0.03
			Sum	2.61	2.88

Table 6.
Calculation of the PEF of electricity mix for Slovenia for 2017, using the reference values from the standard SIST EN 15603.

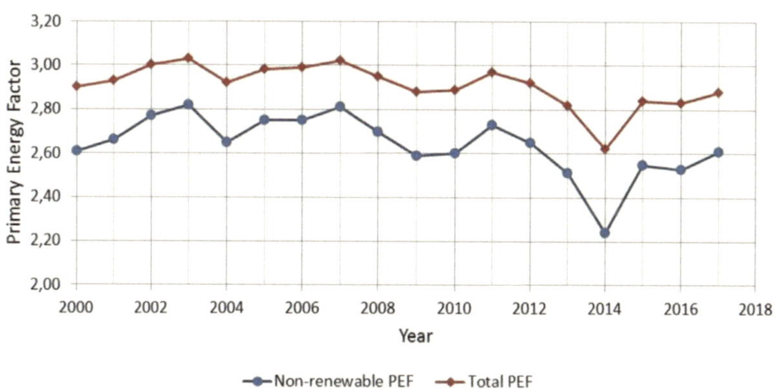

Figure 3.
Average PEFs for nonrenewable and total PE calculated in accordance with SIST EN 15603.

In **Table 6**, two PEFs for the electric mixture are calculated through the fractions of individual energies composing the electricity mix in Slovenia for 2017. We can see that the average PEF for nonrenewable is less than the total factor. The reason for this is that the default primary factors that take into account only the nonrenewable part of primary energy are lower than the total or total factor. The difference between the two average factors is almost 0.3, which is not negligible. As with previous methods, here again, the calculation was also performed for previous years, with the same default factors. The results are shown in **Figure 3**.

3. Results and discussion

By comparing the methods, we can find that the calculation after partial substitution yields the same results for each year. This is due to the default efficiency, which is based on certain default values. Since we get the same PEF for the electricity mixture in all years, we cannot see changes in individual years. It is also impossible to predict what will happen to the factor in the coming years. We can see that the factor is 2.78, which represents a higher value than the predicted factor for Slovenia, which is 2.5 [21].

In the case of the physical energy method, we can better categorize individual years, and from the calculations, we see the PEF fluctuation. Physical energy method assumes energy conversion efficiency of 100% for renewable sources (produced electricity equals primary energy). The highest value of the factor occurred in 2003, while the lowest value amounted to 2.23 in 2016. The reason for such a change in the last year is in the increased production of electricity from renewable sources.

In the last method proposed by the standard SIST EN 15603, which computes two factors, we can see that in the case of the total factor, the value is higher than the average PEF, which takes into account only the nonrenewable part of energy. This is the case for renewable energy sources where PEF values are lower by threefold in comparison to nonrenewable energy sources. What is logical is that we do not consume any energy for the generation of hydro, wind, and solar energy. Likewise, we can also notice here that both factors are the highest in 2003, while they are the lowest in 2014. The reason for this is that the share of produced electricity from fossil fuels is the lowest, and the share of water energy is the highest, which means that due to the low share of energy from fossil fuels and high energy from renewable energy, the factor of PE has decreased.

3.1 Forecast of electricity generation and impact on PEF

By analyzing statistical data and calculating the PEF, we can predict the change of PEF for the electricity mix of Slovenia. The total production of electricity for the coming years and the annual growth of production were calculated by adding the individual quantities of electricity that were calculated by linear regression for each source separately. This means that we added the predicted production of electricity from nuclear power, fossil fuels, hydroelectric power, wind energy, and solar energy. With this simple linear regression, we predicted the amount of energy produced from different sources and how it affects the PEF. The predictions were made for 2020, 2030, and 2040 (**Table 7**). The share of individual sources and the total share of renewables are shown in **Table 8**.

In **Table 8**, we see that the nuclear energy share will decrease over time as well as for fossil fuels, whose share will decrease by more than 5% by 2040. In the case of hydro energy, the share will increase by just over 7%. Wind energy already

Year	2017	2020	2030	2040
Nuclear	6285	6147	6574	7001
Fossil	5610	5592	5524	5455
Hydro	4141	5350	6384	7418
Wind	6	9	14	25
Solar	283	475	894	1312
Total	16,325	17,574	19,392	21,211

Table 7.
Forecast of total electricity production [GWh].

Year	2017	2020	2030	2040
Nuclear	38.5	35.0	33.9	33.0
Fossil	34.36	31.8	28.5	25.7
Hydro	25.37	30.4	32.9	35.0
Wind	0.04	0.1	0.1	0.1
Solar	1.73	2.7	4.6	6.2
Total share of renewables	27.1	33.2	37.6	41.3

Table 8.
Prediction of energy shares in the production of electricity.

represents a very small share in electricity, so in the future it is not expected to grow significantly. The share of solar energy will also increase; by 2040, we can expect an almost 5% increase. As we can see, Slovenia already generates a large share of electricity from renewable sources; by 2040, we can expect that this share will grow by almost 15%.

3.2 Forecast of the primary energy factor for Slovenia

For the partial substitution method, we used the same production efficiency as given in **Table 3**. The only difference is that in this case we carry out the calculation for 2020, 2030, and 2040. In **Table 9** we see an example of the calculation for 2020, where we used the previously predicted quantity of produced electricity.

The PEF calculated according to the method of partial substitution method does not change over the years. The reason why the factor remains the same is that the method assumes the same production efficiency for all energy sources.

For the physical energy method, we used the same production efficiency as in Chapter 2.2. The predictions for 2020, 2030, and 2040 have been recalculated, taking into account the energy production predicted by linear regression. In this method we also considered 10% network losses in the network. The forecasts of the PEF are listed in **Table 10**.

	Production [GWh]	Network loss [GWh]	Useful energy [GWh]	Primary energy [GWh]	PEF
Total	17,574	1757.4	15,816	43,934	2.78

Table 9.
Calculation of predicted PEF by partial substitution method for the production of electricity in Slovenia in 2020.

Year	Production [GWh]	Primary energy [GWh]	PEF
2020	17,574	38,442	2.43
2030	19,392	41,024	2.35
2040	21,211	43,607	2.23

Table 10.
Forecast of the PEF for the electricity mix in Slovenia using the physical energy method.

We can see that the PEF will decrease over time. This result is logical, since the share of renewable energy sources will increase substantially over time. Hence, the PEF is expected to decrease. For better transparency, the PEF calculated by the physical energy method is depicted along its forecast in **Figure 4**.

Calculation of PEF according to the standard SIST EN 15603 was carried out as described in Chapter 2.3. In this method we use the proportions of individual sources determined by linear regression. Two PEFs are proposed, namely, the average PEF-nonrenewable and average PEF-total. The PEFs for 2020 are given in **Table 11**. The average PEF for the electricity mix with predicted values is illustrated in **Figure 5**. It can be noticed that by 2040, the average PEF for nonrenewable energy will decrease to a value of 2.17, while the average PEF-total will be 2.58.

According to the conversion factors of PE, discrepancy between nonrenewable and total PEFs for the electricity mix can be significant. From **Figure 6**, we can see the annual progress of all the PEFs, calculated with all three evaluated methods, for electricity in Slovenia.

With the partial substitution method, we can see that the PEF for electricity does not change over the years, i.e., it remains 2.78. The reason for this lies in the assumption about the efficiency of production from renewable energy sources and nuclear energy, where 40% efficiency is taken into account. Furthermore, the same efficiency is also used for fossil fuels. Therefore, the efficiency of production from all primary sources is 40%. This is why we get the same PEF for all years. This means that according to this method, we do not get the correct representation of the PEF for the electricity mix, or the assumptions are not applicable for the case of Slovenia. In the event that Slovenia produced part of the electricity from biomass, whose production efficiency is estimated with 30% in this method, the PEF would be more volatile. However, Slovenia does not use biomass for the production of electricity; therefore, this method does not give us the useful values of the factor. We also notice that the factor 2.78 is quite high in terms of other methods.

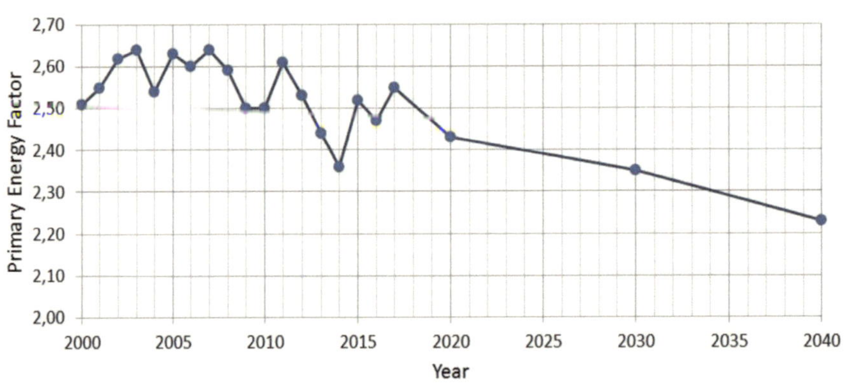

Figure 4.
PEF of electricity calculated according to the physical energy method.

2020	PEF				
	Nonrenewable	Total	Slovenia (average)		
			Energy Share [%]	Nonrenewable	Total
Nuclear	2.8	2.8	34.98	0.98	0.98
Fossil	4.05	4.05	31.82	1.29	1.29
Hydro	0.5	1.5	30.45	0.15	0.46
Wind	0.5	1.5	0.05	0.00	0.00
Solar	0.5	1.5	2.70	0.01	0.04
			Sum	2.43	2.77

Table 11.
Forecast of the PEF for the electricity mix in Slovenia for 2020, using the reference values from the standard SIST EN 15603.

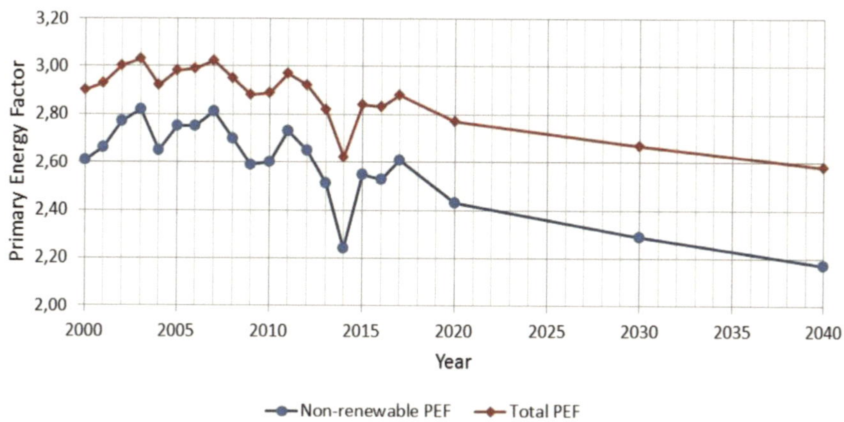

Figure 5.
Average PEF for electricity mix according to the SIST EN 15603 method with predicted values.

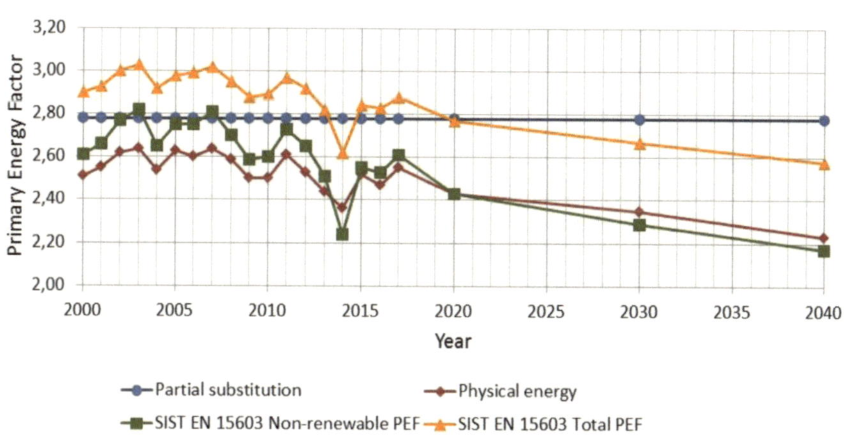

Figure 6.
Comparison of the methods of calculating the PEF for the electricity mix in Slovenia.

The other method used to determine the PEF for electricity is the physical energy method. With this method we evaluate the efficiency of production from renewable energy sources as 100%, while the default efficiency of nuclear power generation and fossil fuel is 33 and 40%, respectively. The PEF calculated according to this method is very low, as shown in **Figure 4**. The reason is in the assumption that the efficiency of production from renewable sources is 100% and Slovenia has a large share of renewable sources in its electricity production, mainly from hydropower sources. In the previous analyses of individual years and forecasts, we also noticed that the share of renewable resources is increasing over time. For this reason, from **Figure 4** decreasing trend for the future is clear. This means that a PEF determined by this method will slowly decrease with respect to the increase in renewable energy sources in electricity generation.

With calculation according to the standard SIST EN 15603, we calculated two different primary energy factors: the average PEF for nonrenewables, which takes into account only the nonrenewable part of the energy of individual primary sources, and the PEF, which takes into account the total share of primary energies. We used the default values of the individual factors determined by the method for each primary source separately. We can see that the average PEF for nonrenewable energy is much lower than the total. The reason for this is that the default values of the factors that we use to calculate the nonrenewable and total factor are different. The greatest differences occur in renewable energy sources. This is because renewable energy sources have a very small share of nonrenewable energy. Therefore, the factors for calculating the individual PE sources are low in the case of hydropower, wind, and solar energy. When calculating the total factor, the factor value for these types of energy is 1.5. Moreover, a different calculation approach is used in this method, i.e., the PEF is calculated through the shares of individual energy sources in the total electricity.

4. Conclusions

PEFs are used to describe the conversion efficiency from primary energy sources to secondary energy sources, which are supplied to end consumers. PEFs are, therefore, used for comparing necessary quantities of primary energy to the final energy demands. At EU level as well as national levels, PEFs are used for converting final energy to primary energy consumption, for comparing efficiency of devices with different energy sources as well as to benchmark building energy performance. As it stands, the EU Member States can autonomously determine national PEFs, which in turn can skew the evaluation process of primary energy use in buildings.

We analyzed the three most commonly used methods used to determine the PEF for the electricity mix. We examined what are the assumptions of the individual methods and the individual default values that the method assumes. Then, using these methods, the value of the PEF for electricity in Slovenia was determined. We also recalculated with all the methods how the PEF changed over time at an annual level. All calculations were made using statistical data about produced electricity from various primary energy sources and individual assumptions determined by the methods. In addition, a statistical analysis using linear regression was carried out in order to predict the future PEF values for all three considered methods.

We have found that the methods differ in the evaluation of individual primary sources, which has a significant impact on the PEF value. In addition, we observed that the factor is also changing in terms of the electricity production from different sources, which means that the factor depends on the amount of energy that is produced either from nonrenewable sources of energy or from renewable energy sources. If the annual production of electricity from renewable energy sources is higher, we can expect a lower PEF and vice versa. We also noted that the share of renewable resources increases over time, which is also noticeable in the predicted values of production from renewable energy sources.

We also found that with the partial substitution method, we do not get representative results about the PEF, since it remains constant over the years. This means that this method does not provide a proper representation of the PEFs and, hence, is not applicable for the case in Slovenia. The method of physical energy gives the efficiency of production from renewable energy sources as 100%. Here, too, the question arises as to whether the evaluation is completely correct and if we can truly assume that the use of PE is equal to the actual production of electricity. In the third method, defined in the standard SIST EN 15603, which provides two PEFs, a certain measure of criticality of the assumed factors for the different sources of energy is used.

Author details

Matjaž Prek
Faculty of Mechanical Engineering, University of Ljubljana, Ljubljana, Slovenia

*Address all correspondence to: matjaz.prek@fs.uni-lj.si

References

[1] Directive 2010/31/EU of European Parliament and of the Council of 19 May 2010 on the Energy Performance of Buildings (Recast). 2010. http://eur-lex.europa.eu/LexUriServ/LexUriServ.do?uri=OJ:L:2010:153:0013:0035:en:PDF

[2] Directive 2012/27/EU of the European Parliament and of the Council of 25 October 2012 On Energy Efficiency, Amending Directives 2009/125/EC and 2010/30/EU and Repealing Directives 2004/8/EC and 2006/32/EC. 2012. https://eur-lex.europa.eu/LexUriServ/LexUriServ.do?uri=OJ:L:2012:315:0001:0056:en:PDF

[3] Directive 2009/125/EC of the European Parliament and of the Council of 21 October 2009 Establishing a Framework for the Setting of Eco-Design Requirements for Energy-Related Products. https://eur-lex.europa.eu/LexUriServ/LexUriServ.do?uri=OJ:L:2009:285:0010:0035:en:PDF

[4] Regulation EU 2017/1369 of the European Parliament and of the Council of 4 July 2017 Setting a Framework for Energy Labelling and Repealing Directive 2010/30/EU. https://eur-lex.europa.eu/legal-content/EN/TXT/PDF/?uri=CELEX:32017R1369&rid=7

[5] Directive 2009/28/EC of the European Parliament and of the Council of 23 April 2009 on the Promotion of the Use of Energy from Renewable Sources and Amending and Subsequently Repealing Directives 2001/77/EC and 2003/30/EC. https://eur-lex.europa.eu/legal-content/EN/TXT/PDF/?uri=CELEX:32009L0028&rid=8

[6] Taner T, Sivrioglu M. Data on energy, exergy analysis and optimisation for a sugar factory. Data in Brief. 2015;5:408-410. DOI: 10.1016/j.dib.2015.09.028

[7] Taner T, Sivrioglu M. Energy-exergy analysis and optimisation of a model sugar factory in Turkey. Energy. 2015;**93**:641-654. DOI: 10.1016/j.energy.2015.09.007

[8] Taner T. Energy and exergy analyze of PEM fuel cell: A case study of modeling and simulations. Energy. 2018;**143**:284-294. DOI: 10.1016/j.energy.2017.10.102

[9] Taner T. Exergy analysis of a circulating fluidized bed power plant co-firing with olive pits: A case study of power plant in Turkey. Energy. 2017;**140**:40-46. DOI: 10.1016/j.energy.2017.08.042

[10] Taner T. Optimisation processes of energy efficiency for a drying plant: A case of study for Turkey. Applied Thermal Engineering. 2015;**80**:247-260. DOI: 10.1016/j.applthermaleng.2015.01.076

[11] Taner T, Sivrioglu M. A techno-economic & cost analysis of a turbine power plant: A case study for sugar plant. Renewable and Sustainable Energy Reviews. 2017;**78**:722-730. DOI: 10.1016/j.rser.2017.04.104

[12] ANSI/ASHRAE Standard 105-2014. Standard Method of Determining, Expressing and Comparing Building Energy Performance and Greenhouse Gas Emission. Atlanta, USA: ASHRAE; 2014

[13] Directive (EU) 2018/844 of the European Parliament and of the Council of 30 May 2018 Amending Directive 2010/31/EU on the Energy Performance of Buildings and Directive 2012/27/EU on Energy Efficiency. https://eur-lex.europa.eu/legal-content/EN/TXT/PDF/?uri=CELEX:32018L0844&from=IT

[14] ISO 52000-1:2017. Energy performance of buildings—Overarching

EPB assessment—Part 1: General framework and procedures. Geneva: International Organization for Standardization; 2017

[15] SIST EN 15603:2008. Energy performance of buildings—Overall energy use and definitions of energy ratings. Brussels: European Committee for Standardization; 2008

[16] Statistični Urad Republike Slovenije: Električna Energija (GWh). Slovenija. Available from: https://pxweb.stat.si/pxweb/Dialog/varval.asp?ma=1817602S&ti=&path=../Database/Okolje/18_energetika/03_18176_elektricna_energija/&lang=2

[17] Segers R. Three options to calculate the percentage renewable energy: An example for a EU policy debate. Energy Policy. 2008;**36**:3243-3248. DOI: 10.1016/j.enpol.2008.05.014

[18] Conversion Factors for Electricity in Energy Policy. A Review of Regulatory Application of Conversion Factors for Electricity and an Assessment of their Impact on EU Energy and Climate Goals. Norway: ADAPT Consulting a.s.; 2013

[19] IEA (International Energy Agency). Energy Statistics Manual. France: IED Publications; 2005

[20] Eurostat: Definition of the Primary Energy Content of Fuels. Available from: https://ec.europa.eu/eurostat/statistics-explained/index.php/Calculation_methodologies_for_the_share_of_renewables_in_energy_consumption#Definition_of_the_primary_energy_content_of_fuels

[21] Tehnična Smernica TSG-1-004:2010. Učinkovita Raba Energije. Slovenia: Ministrstvo za Okolje in Prostor; 2010. Available from: http://www.mop.gov.si/fileadmin/mop.gov.si/pageuploads/zakonodaja/graditev_objektov/TSG_01_004_2010_ure.pdf

Section 3

Energy Application for Country

Chapter 5

Determinants of Energy Demand Efficiency: Evidence from Japan's Industrial Sector

Akihiro Otsuka

Abstract

With the growing demand for energy, improving energy efficiency has become a key policy issue in Japan. Therefore, this study estimates the energy demand function of Japan's industrial sector using a stochastic frontier model and analyzes the level of energy efficiency and its determinants. An empirical analysis based on the data of 47 Japanese prefectures presents three main findings. First, installment in large production facilities deteriorates energy efficiency and second, it is effective in increasing the electrification rate to improve energy efficiency. Finally, improving productivity leads to an increase in the electrification rate. These results suggest that policies aimed at increasing electrification by enhancing the productivity of factories and offices significantly contribute to improving energy efficiency.

Keywords: energy efficiency, industrial sector, electrification rate, stochastic frontier analysis, Japan

1. Introduction

Technological modernization is one of the key elements of success in improving productivity and environmental management [1]. It has advanced in power plants and as a result, energy efficiency has increased. Regarding plant efficiency, there are numerous findings from the engineering viewpoint [2, 3]. Research on fuel cells is also active, Taner [4] measuring the energy efficiency of the proton exchange membrane fuel cell. Based on these technical studies, this chapter focuses on the efficiency of the overall energy demand in a country and region, not the individual efficiencies of plants and technology unit. In other words, this study analyzes the energy consumption efficiency from an economic viewpoint. Energy consumption is primary and secondary, or final energy consumption. The focus of this study is final energy demand efficiency.

Energy consumption is mainly affected by energy efficiency. Given the current trend in Japan, the energy saving in the manufacturing sector as a subsector of the industrial sector has strengthened, given the drastic improvements in the energy efficiency of factory facilities. However, in the commercial sector as another subsector of the industrial sector, energy saving has deteriorated and this, in turn, has increased energy consumption. Japan's industrial sector accounts for a large proportion of the nation's energy consumption, and thus, increasing the energy efficiency of this sector has become a key policy issue.

There is no clear and accepted definition of energy efficiency, but according to Bhattacharyya [5], most definitions are based on a simple ratio of "useful output of a process/energy input into a process." Additionally, Patterson [6] shows several ways to quantify the output and input of this ratio. One of the ratios most frequently used in energy analysis at the macro level is the energy-GDP ratio, called energy intensity, which is in fact the reciprocal of the economic-thermodynamic index of energy efficiency identified by Patterson [6]. Energy intensity has been traditionally used as an indicator of energy efficiency. However, this approach has been disputed by the claims that energy intensity may not reflect the specific factors that enable energy intensity to accurately approximate energy efficiency [7–9]. An Energy Information Administration (EIA) [7] report first highlighted that energy intensity and efficiency are often used interchangeably and discussed the use of energy intensity as a measure of energy efficiency. Energy intensity is thus susceptible to socioeconomic factors other than energy efficiency, such as energy price, income, and production environment. Given this energy intensity problem, we need to control other important factors to obtain a pure measure of energy efficiency. Therefore, numerous studies attempted to measure the energy efficiency indices by conducting stochastic frontier analysis (SFA) and data envelopment analysis (DEA).

For instance, Huntington [10] discusses the relationship between energy and production efficiency using the framework of production theory. Feijoo et al. [11] conduct SFA to measure the energy efficiency of Spanish industries and Buck and Young [12] to estimate the energy efficiency of commercial buildings in Canada. Similarly, Boyd [13] analyzes the energy efficiency of wet corn milling plants and highlights the advantage of not having to define the problem of energy intensity in an SFA. Further, Zhou and Ang [14] measure the energy efficiency of 21 OECD countries using DEA. On the other hand, Filippini and Hunt measure the energy efficiency of 29 OECD countries [15] and calculate the energy efficiency of the US household sector using SFA [16]. The authors show that the energy efficiency level measured by conducting an SFA is not correlated with energy intensity, thus concluding that energy intensity is not a suitable proxy for energy efficiency. Carvalho [17] follows a time frame similar to that of Filippini and Hunt [15] and covers a series of non-OECD countries. Aranda-Uson et al. [18] perform an SFA to measure the energy efficiency for Spain's grocery and tobacco manufacturing, textile, chemical, and nonferrous metal product manufacturing industries. China-based studies have also applied SFA to measure the energy efficiency of the thermal power [19], iron and steel, and chemical industries [20, 21]. Lin and Du [22] and Filippini and Lin [23] compare energy efficiency levels across Chinese provinces using various econometric models, including SFA.

In sum, numerous studies support the use of an SFA instead of energy intensity as an indicator of energy efficiency. Moreover, SFA is a parametric approach that can tackle statistical noise and thus, is more desirable than DEA, a nonparametric approach. To this effect, Zhou et al. [24] evaluate the energy efficiency index using both approaches and show SFA is more desirable than DEA. A large body of research focuses on measuring energy efficiency values using SFA, whereas few studies explore the individual factors determining energy efficiency levels, such as the empirical works by Otsuka [25, 26]. These studies analyze the energy consumption trends of households and reveal that resident characteristics determine energy and electricity efficiency. However, to the best of the author's knowledge, there is a scarcity of research on economic production sectors. Particularly, how mechanization and electrification affect the energy efficiency have not been clarified.

This study thus measures the level of energy efficiency by using SFA and clarifies the determinants of the improvements in energy efficiency for Japan's industrial sector. Specifically, it focuses on two factors influencing the energy efficiency of the industrial sector. The first is the capital-labor ratio, that is, "mechanization," wherein installing large intensive machinery equipment deteriorates energy efficiency. Conversely, the installation of compact and dispersed production facilities is expected to increase the energy efficiency. The second factor is the electrification rate. Advancing the electrification of factories and offices is directly linked to greater operational productivity and thus, the possibility of increasing energy efficiency.

Porter and van der Linde [27] highlight that improving productivity throughout the production process under appropriate environmental regulations could relatively reduce energy usage and, consequently, increase the energy efficiency. Boyd and Pang [28] and Otsuka et al. [29] also empirically demonstrate that productivity gain improves energy efficiency, that is, energy efficiency serves as a guidepost for improving productivity. Drawing on these works, this study verifies the hypothesis that productivity improvements under environmental constraints are compatible with those in energy efficiency.

The remainder of this study is organized as follows. Section 2 describes the empirical analysis framework, as well as the models and data. Section 3 presents the empirical results, followed by an analysis of the findings. Section 4 concludes the study.

2. Materials and methods

2.1 Econometric model for energy efficiency

This study assumes the following aggregated energy demand function, f, exists at the Japanese prefectural level. That is,

$$E_{jt} = f(P_t, Y_{jt}, KL_{jt}, IK_{jt}, CDD_{jt}, HDD_{jt}, EF_{jt}) \tag{1}$$

where j denotes a region ($j = 1, \ldots, J$), t is time ($t = 1, \ldots, T$) and E is the final energy consumption for the industrial sector. P is the energy price index for the sector and Y income. KL is the capital-labor ratio and represents the degree of mechanization in a factory or office. Thompson and Taylor [30] show that capital and energy both have short- and long-term relationships. IK is the proportion of investment in capital stock and represents the degree of vintage. CDD and HDD are the cooling and heating degree days and represent temperature. In regions with severe temperatures, energy consumption is more likely to be associated with air conditioning. Previous studies have shown that CDD and HDD, as indicators of cooling and heating, are related to energy consumption [31, 32]. EF is the level of energy efficiency in a region.

It is necessary to estimate energy efficiency, particularly because it is not directly observable in an economic system. Therefore, this study estimates energy efficiency using a stochastic frontier energy demand function. Stochastic frontier functions generally measure the economic performance of production and operation processes and have therefore been applied to production or cost theory using an econometric approach. This approach is based on the notion that frontier functions produce the maximum output or minimum cost levels achievable by a producer. In a production function, the frontier represents the maximum production level for a given input. In a cost function, the frontier is the minimum cost for a given output. An energy demand function can thus be considered similar to a cost function. In other words, the difference between observed energy demand and minimized demand is the technical inefficiency observed when the output for a production activity is given. In an aggregate energy demand function, the frontier denotes the minimum energy level needed for the production activities in a region to achieve a given production level. In other words, by estimating an energy demand frontier function, it is possible to determine the baseline energy demand that reflects the energy demand in a region that is efficiently managing energy use through its production and operational processes. Additionally, it allows us to ascertain whether a region is on the frontier. If a region is not on the frontier, the distance from the frontier indicates the rate of energy consumption exceeding baseline demand (i.e., energy inefficiency) [33].

The panel SFA in this study follows the premise of Aigner et al. [34]. Further, this study adopts the one-step approach of Battese and Coelli [35]. It thus estimates the energy frontier function and the determinants of the energy inefficiency term simultaneously. Traditionally, a two-step estimation method is adopted, in which inefficiency is obtained by estimating the stochastic frontier function, and the value is regressed by determinants. In this case, a contradiction arises between the assumption of the distribution on the inefficiency term of the frontier function and the regression analyzing the inefficiency determinant. As such, the consistency of the estimation result is not guaranteed [36]. By adopting the one-step approach, we can avoid this problem. An SFA model using this approach approximates an economy's energy efficiency level based on a one-sided non-negative error term. That is, this study assumes the log-log function type in Eq. (1) can be specified as follows:

$$\begin{aligned} \ln E_{jt} &= \alpha + \alpha_P \ln P_t + \alpha_Y \ln Y_{jt} + \alpha_{KL} \ln KL_{jt} + \alpha_{IK} \ln IK_{jt} \\ &+ \alpha_{CDD} \ln CDD_{jt} + \alpha_{HDD} \ln HDD_{jt} + v_{jt} + u_{jt}, \end{aligned} \tag{2}$$

where α is an estimated parameter. The error term $(v_{jt} + u_{jt})$ consists of two parts, a random error term v_{jt} and an error term for inefficiency, u_{jt}. It is assumed that v_{jt} has a distribution $N(0, \sigma^2)$ and is independent of u_{jt} and all explanatory variables. u_{jt} is a non-negative random variable and follows the distribution $N(\mu, \sigma_u^2)$. u_{jt} indicates that the efficiency energy level EF in Eq. (1) is an energy inefficiency index. Given Eq. (2), the energy efficiency level EF_{jt} is estimated using the conditional expectation $E(u_{jt}|v_{jt} + u_{jt})$ for the efficiency term [37]. Specifically, the energy efficiency level EF_{jt} is measured by the ratio of the estimated energy demand frontier E_{jt}^F to the observed energy demand E_{jt}. In other words, $EF_{jt} \equiv E_{jt}^F / E_{jt} = e^{-u_{jt}}, 0 < EF_{jt} \leq 1$.

Improvements in energy efficiency can be achieved through social innovation in the production and consumption processes of energy services, as well as the technical and organizational factors of energy demand. Average energy efficiency in this study is formulated as:

$$\mu_{jt} = \beta + \beta_{KL} \ln KL_{jt} + \beta_{ER} \ln ER_{jt}, \tag{3}$$

where β is an estimated parameter, KL is the capital-labor ratio, and ER is the electrification rate for the industrial sector. If the factor of the inefficiency term improves the efficiency, the sign of β is negative.

Factories and offices with large-scale facilities have high energy consumption and low energy efficiency in production. For example, a petrochemical complex, the paper pulp manufacturing industry, and the steel industry have large-scale production facilities. Therefore, the energy efficiency levels of these industries are low. Meanwhile, labor-intensive factories and offices have compact-scale production facilities, thus low energy consumption and high energy efficiency. For example, labor-intensive process-assembled industries are more energy efficient than material-based industries [38]. To control the differences in local production industries, this study considers capital-labor ratio. The coefficient values for *KL* are expected to be positive.

Regions that use coal and kerosene tend to report higher carbon dioxide emissions than those using electricity. Further, areas with a low electrification rate are considered wasteful in terms of energy use. Electrification of factories and offices enables an efficient use of energy. For example, a factory energy management system (FEMS) can be introduced to electrify a factory. A FEMS functions in coordination with power generation, power storage, and energy saving devices, allowing for energy saving that industries have been unable to hitherto realize. Furthermore, the implementation of a building energy management system (BEMS) for commercial buildings could reduce energy consumption and control energy-related facilities. Consequently, energy efficiency could increase with a rise in electricity usage through promoting electrification. Therefore, the coefficient values for *ER* are expected to be negative.

2.2 Determinant model for the electrification rate

Electrification can significantly influence the improvement of energy efficiency in a region. Therefore, this study conducts a quantitative analysis as an additional regression that account for the characteristics of factories and offices that may be electrification determinants.

The variables in the following equation are assumed to be determinants of a region's electrification rate:

$$\begin{aligned}\ln ER_{jt} &= \delta_{LN}\ln LN_{jt} + \delta_{OR}\ln OR_{jt} + \delta_{TFP}\ln TFP_{jt} + \delta_{CDD}\ln CDD_{jt} \\ &\quad + \delta_{HDD}\ln HDD_{jt} + \delta_j + \varepsilon_{jt},\end{aligned} \tag{4}$$

where j is a region (j = 1, ..., J), t is the time (t = 1, ..., T), *ER* is the electrification rate in the industrial sector, and *LN is* the number of employees per establishment, comprising offices and factories, and denotes the scale of an establishment. *OR* is the ratio of the number of offices to that of establishments; *TFP* is the total factor productivity and represents an establishment's productivity level; *CDD* and *HDD* are cooling and heating degree days, respectively; and δ is an estimated parameter. Since this study uses panel data, δj denotes the fixed effect. In estimation of (4), it is necessary to consider endogeneity between the productivity and the electrification rate. It would be possible that a higher electrification rate also influences productivity. Although these endogeneity effects can be treated with a fixed effect model, it is not sufficient. To obtain robust results, this study calculates the estimates by panel GMM using instrumental variables in addition to the fixed effect model.

2.3 Data

The data used for the analysis are 1990–2010 panel data for 47 prefectures. Data on the final energy consumption (*E*) of the sectors of each prefecture are taken from the Energy Consumption Statistics by Prefecture (Ministry of Economy, Trade, and Industry). The energy price index (*P*) is estimated using the real energy price index for the respective sector by the International Energy Agency (IEA). Income (*Y*) is a real gross regional expenditure, data for which are available in the Annual Report on Prefectural Accounts (Cabinet Office). The capital-labor ratio (*KL*) is the ratio of capital stock to the number of employees, and data for the number of employed persons are available in the Annual Report on Prefectural Accounts

Description	Variable	Mean	Std. dev.	Maximum	Minimum
Final energy consumption (TJ)	E	199,829	214,836	1,181,999	24,530
Energy price index (2010 = 100)	P	86.5	8.9	111.5	77.7
Income (JPY, millions)	Y	10,422,755	14,063,661	100,931,767	1,865,830
Capital-labor ratio	KL	15.48	3.51	26.19	7.27
Vintage	IK	0.061	0.016	0.118	0.035
Cooling degree day	CDD	367.0	175.6	1186.1	0.0
Heating degree day	HDD	1106.3	470.9	2769.2	0.2
Electrification rate (%)	ER	36.18	12.08	59.29	8.55
Establishment size (person)	LN	9.34	0.87	12.12	7.08
Office ratio (%)	OR	94.92	1.62	98.20	89.67
TFP index	TFP	0.185	0.112	0.662	−0.055

Sources: For final energy consumption, see Energy Consumption Statistics by Prefecture (Ministry of Economy, Trade and Industry: http://www.enecho.meti.go.jp/statistics/energy_consumption/ec002/); for energy price index, see International Energy Agency databases; for income, see Annual Report on Prefectural Accounts (Cabinet Office: http://www.esri.cao.go.jp/jp/sna/sonota/kenmin/kenmin_top.html); for capital-labor ratio, see Central Research Institute of Electric Power Industry databases; for vintage, see Central Research Institute of Electric Power Industry databases; for electrification rate, see Energy Consumption Statistics by Prefecture (Ministry of Economy, Trade and Industry: http://www.enecho.meti.go.jp/statistics/energy_consumption/ec002/); for establishment size and office ratio, see Economic Census (Statistics Bureau, Ministry of Internal Affairs and Communications: http://www.stat.go.jp/data/e-census/index.html); and for TFP index, see Otsuka and Goto [29]: https://link.springer.com/article/10.1007/s00168-016-0745-x.

Table 1.
Descriptive statistics.

Panel A							
	Final energy consumption (TJ)	Energy price index (2010 = 100)	Income (JPY, millions)	Capital-labor ratio	Vintage	Cooling degree day	Heating degree day
Region	E	P	Y	KL	IK	CDD	HDD
Hokkaido	322,771	100.00	19,199,451	15.09	0.035	124.0	2591.2
Tohoku	84,446	100.00	5,948,899	18.69	0.042	315.4	1907.7
Kita-Kanto	170,132	100.00	7,908,596	19.67	0.046	450.4	1407.0
Greater Tokyo area	613,806	100.00	41,983,820	19.21	0.046	492.5	1060.9
Chubu	234,453	100.00	14,956,162	21.40	0.046	511.0	1270.3
Hokuriku	55,461	100.00	4,209,377	20.81	0.043	476.2	1522.8
Kansai	211,767	100.00	13,566,039	20.86	0.047	556.5	1116.0
Chugoku	269,740	100.00	5,900,042	20.52	0.045	539.2	1194.3
Shikoku	75,918	100.00	3,549,752	19.05	0.046	572.4	910.6
Kyushu	138,517	100.00	6,618,666	18.32	0.047	545.1	911.8
Okinawa	38,462	100.00	3,850,416	12.97	0.052	909.0	122.2

Panel B				
	Electrification rate (%)	Establishment size (person)	Office ratio (%)	TFP index
Region	ER	LN	OR	TFP
Hokkaido	34.69	9.84	97.67	0.25
Tohoku	44.58	9.27	96.33	0.15
Kita-Kanto	46.78	9.53	95.23	0.27
Greater Tokyo area	30.67	11.08	96.82	0.40
Chubu	44.25	9.70	94.77	0.26
Hokuriku	51.66	8.84	95.00	0.22
Kansai	40.63	9.34	95.82	0.32
Chugoku	28.35	9.53	96.47	0.19
Shikoku	38.06	8.55	96.59	0.21
Kyushu	38.78	9.53	97.13	0.15
Okinawa	49.24	8.24	98.20	0.14

Notes: the regional classification is as follows: Hokkaido (Hokkaido), Tohoku (Aomori, Iwate, Miyagi, Akita, Yamagata, Fukushima, and Niigata), Tokyo (Saitama, Chiba, Tokyo, Kanagawa, Ibaraki, Tochigi, Gunma, and Yamanashi), Hokuriku (Toyama, Ishikawa, and Fukui), Chubu (Nagano, Gifu, Shizuoka, Aichi, and Mie), Kansai (Shiga, Kyoto, Osaka, Hyogo, Nara, and Wakayama), Chugoku (Tottori, Shimane, Okayama, Hiroshima, and Yamaguchi), Shikoku (Tokushima, Kagawa, Ehime, and Kochi), Kyushu (Fukuoka, Saga, Nagasaki, Kumamoto, Oita, Miyazaki, and Kagoshima), and Okinawa (Okinawa).

Table 2.
Regional characteristics for Japan (as of 2010).

(Cabinet Office). Capital vintage (*IK*) is the ratio of capital investment to capital stock. Data on capital investment and stock are based on the data published by the Central Research Institute of Electric Power Industry. Data on *CDD* and *HDD* are from the prefectural government's location and weather station—cooling degree day is the sum of the difference between average temperature on the days exceeding 24 and 22°C, while heating degree day is the sum of the difference between average temperatures below 14°C and above 14°C. The *ER* is estimated from the data in the Energy Consumption Statistics by Prefecture (Ministry of Economy, Trade, and Industry). The estimation for the percentage of offices for all establishments (*OR*) is based on the number of business establishments listed by the Economic Census (Ministry of Economy, Trade, and Industry). Data for productivity (*TFP*) are the total factor productivity calculated by Otsuka and Goto [39]. **Table 1** presents the descriptive statistics.

Table 2 presents the regional characteristics for Japan as of 2010. Particularly, large metropolitan areas, such as the Greater Tokyo Area, Kansai, and Chubu, report high energy consumption. Moreover, the income scale is large and vintage is high in these areas. The capital-labor ratio is relatively high because the manufacturing industry is concentrated in the Chubu and Hokuriku regions. The degree of air conditioning usage is significant in the warm western Japan, and the number of heating days is high in eastern Japan. Further, the Greater Tokyo Area, Kansai, and Chubu have several large-scale business establishments and productivity tends to be high here.

3. Results and discussion

Table 3 presents the estimation results for the energy demand frontier function. Model A shows the estimation results of (2) and (3). Model B shows the estimation result of the model considering a nonlinear effect in the inefficiency determinant.

First, let us consider the results of Model A. The estimated coefficients show the expected signs, and all variables are statistically significant. Since each variable is a logarithmic variable, the estimated parameter can be interpreted as elasticity. Estimated price elasticity is 0.046 and income elasticity 0.707, indicating that income elasticity significantly exceeds price elasticity. Price elasticity is inelastic and denotes the nature of energy goods as essential goods. The capital-labor ratio and the coefficient on vintage are positive and have reasonable signs. This suggests that there is more energy demand in areas where industries for which mechanization is progressing are located. It also shows that capital investment increases energy demand. The coefficients for cooling degree day are slightly significant, but their magnitude is small. Additionally, the coefficients for heating degree day are not significant. These results show that temperature is a weak determinant of energy demand in the industrial sector.

Next, this study evaluates the estimation results for the factors determining energy efficiency. The capital-labor ratio is positive and reports the expected sign. This indicates that energy efficiency deteriorates with an increase in mechanization. In other words, energy efficiency is lower in regions where numerous industries with large-scale facilities are located. The electrification rate is negative, reporting the expected sign. The results show that an increase in the electrification rate enhances energy efficiency. The coefficient value for the electrification rate is considerably larger than that for the capital-labor ratio. That is, the positive impact

	Model A		Model B	
	Coefficient	**Standard error**	**Coefficient**	**Standard error**
Constant (α)	−0.584**	(0.038)	−0.571**	(0.040)
α_P	−0.046**	(0.009)	−0.039**	(0.009)
α_Y	0.707**	(0.010)	0.705**	(0.010)
α_{KL}	0.10 **	(0.023)	0.109**	(0.021)
α_{IK}	0.065**	(0.010)	0.073**	(0.011)
α_{CDD}	−0.021*	(0.009)	−0.021*	(0.009)
α_{HDD}	−0.005	(0.007)	−0.006	(0.007)
Constant (β)	0.534**	(0.043)	0.556**	(0.047)
β_{KL}	0.093**	(0.025)	0.096**	(0.024)
β_{KL}^2			−0.028**	(0.009)
β_{ER}	−0.522**	(0.011)	−0.556**	(0.026)
β_{ER}^2			−0.019	(0.011)
$\sigma_u^2 + \sigma_v^2$	0.062**	(0.004)	0.063**	(0.004)
$\sigma_u^2/(\sigma_u^2 + \sigma_v^2)$	0.692**	(0.096)	0.690**	(0.092)
Number of observations	987		987	

*Note: ** and * denote significance at the 1 and 5% levels, respectively.*

Table 3.
Estimation results for 1980–2010.

of installing power facilities and an increase in the electrification rate from office automation are more significant than the negative impact of installing large productive capital equipment.

Due to these effects, this study estimates Model B, which account for the nonlinear effects of determinants. Statistically, significant values are obtained for the quadratic term of the capital-labor ratio. The sign of the quadratic term is negative. This shows there is a threshold for the impact of the capital-labor ratio on energy efficiency. Specifically, the increase in mechanization improves energy efficiency, but it exacerbates energy efficiency when it exceeds a threshold value. On the other hand, the quadratic terms for electrification are not statistically significant, and the nonlinear effects of electrification are not recognizable.

During the observation period (1990–2010), there was financial crisis in 2008. As the economic depression spreads worldwide from the US, Japan's economic growth rate fell greatly in 2008. This economic downturn had a significant influence on the production system of the regional industry. Hence, when considering result stability, this influence must be considered. Therefore, the analysis period is reset from 1990 to 2007, and Model A and Model B reestimated. **Table 4** shows the reestimation results. Model C represents the result of reestimation of Model A and Model D of Model B. There is no significant difference in the regression coefficients in **Table 4**. Therefore, the results in **Table 3** can be judged as robust.

Table 5 presents the descriptive statistics for the energy efficiency values of each prefecture, obtained from the estimation results (Model A). An efficiency value of 1 denotes the highest efficiency, while a value below 1 indicates lower energy efficiency. The average energy efficiency value is 0.617 and the median value 0.685. More importantly, a maximum value of 0.950 and a minimum of

	Model C		Model D	
	Coefficient	**Standard error**	**Coefficient**	**Standard error**
Constant (α)	−0.577**	(0.044)	−0.576**	(0.049)
α_P	−0.063**	(0.014)	−0.056**	(0.014)
α_Y	0.709**	(0.011)	0.706 **	(0.011)
α_{KL}	0.121**	(0.027)	0.118**	(0.027)
α_{IK}	0.073**	(0.012)	0.079**	(0.012)
α_{CDD}	−0.018	(0.009)	−0.018	(0.009)
α_{HDD}	−0.006	(0.008)	−0.008	(0.007)
Constant (β)	0.520**	(0.051)	0.552**	(0.058)
β_{KL}	0.094**	(0.029)	0.091**	(0.029)
β^2_{KL}			−0.028*	(0.010)
β_{ER}	−0.522**	(0.012)	−0.543**	(0.028)
β^2_{ER}			−0.012	(0.012)
$\sigma_u^2 + \sigma_v^2$	0.062 **	(0.004)	0.063**	(0.004)
$\sigma_u^2/(\sigma_u^2 + \sigma_v^2)$	0.648**	(0.111)	0.667**	(0.106)
Number of observations	846		846	

*Note: ** and * denote significance at the 1 and 5% levels, respectively.*

Table 4.
Estimation results for 1980–2007.

Mean	0.617
Std. dev.	0.234
Minimum	0.114
Maximum	0.950
Median	0.685

Note: The energy efficiency scores in the table are calculated using the estimation results for Model A.

Table 5.
Descriptive statistics of energy efficiency scores.

0.114 point to a significant difference in energy efficiency levels among regions. **Figure 1** shows the time-series transition of the national average energy efficiency scores. The average energy efficiency score of Japan's industrial sector has been consistently increasing until 2007, after declining from 1990 to 1994. Energy conservation progressed from the latter half of the 1990s to the 2000s, and energy efficiency thus improved. However, in 2008, energy efficiency worsened and then increased slightly.

Table 6 presents the average energy efficiency scores for each prefecture and ranks them accordingly. Nara, Tokyo, Yamanashi, Ishikawa, Saga, and Yamagata are among the high-ranking areas. The factories and offices located in these areas are likely to report an increasing rate of electrification. On the other hand, Oita has the lowest energy efficiency. Okayama, Chiba, and Yamaguchi have petrochemical complexes and, thus, low energy efficiency, because petrochemical complexes have large-scale production facilities and are lagging in electrification, given the large demands for coal, kerosene, and gas for production.

Table 6 also shows the change rate of the average scores for the energy efficiency between the 1990s and the 2000s. The table highlights two key characteristics. First, Mie, Wakayama, and Fukuoka report improved average scores. Specifically, Mie has the highest improvement score, and its energy efficiency value shows an annual improvement of 1.87%. Wakayama and Fukuoka's scores improve by 1.36 and 1.12%

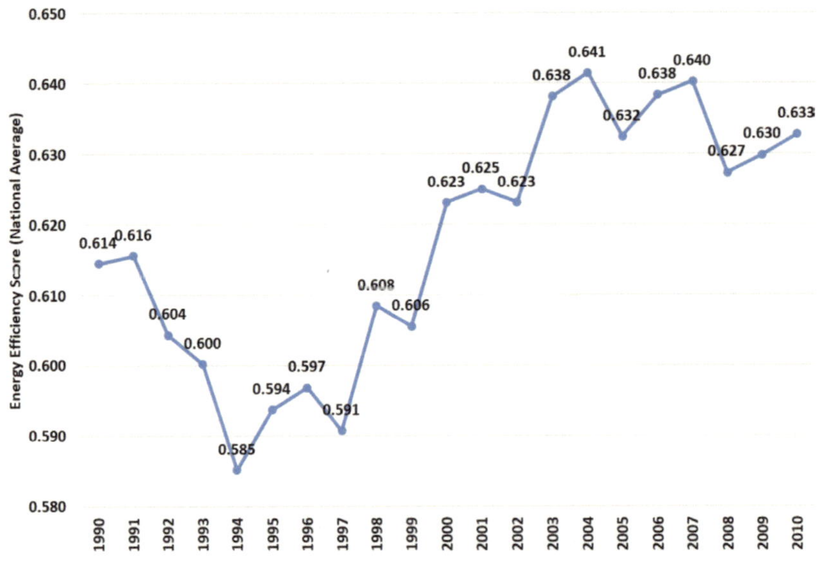

Figure 1.
Time trend of national average energy efficiency scores.

Rank	Prefecture	Average efficiency score	Change rate of score
1	Nara	0.93	−0.22
2	Tokyo	0.92	−0.10
3	Yamanashi	0.91	−0.10
4	Ishikawa	0.90	−0.20
5	Saga	0.87	−0.06
6	Yamagata	0.86	−0.01
7	Nagano	0.86	0.17
8	Kyoto	0.85	−0.19
9	Okinawa	0.84	−0.07
10	Gunma	0.84	0.00
11	Akita	0.84	−0.46
12	Fukui	0.83	−0.01
13	Kumamoto	0.79	−0.38
14	Fukushima	0.79	0.73
15	Shiga	0.77	0.81
16	Shimane	0.77	0.61
17	Tochigi	0.77	−0.18
18	Nagasaki	0.76	0.79
19	Gifu	0.72	−0.13
20	Saitama	0.72	−0.14
21	Kagoshima	0.72	−0.29
22	Tottori	0.71	−1.07
23	Miyagi	0.71	−0.59
24	Iwate	0.68	0.15
25	Toyama	0.67	0.51
26	Shizuoka	0.65	0.81
27	Tokushima	0.64	1.39
28	Miyazaki	0.63	0.82
29	Osaka	0.61	0.16
30	Niigata	0.60	0.11
31	Aichi	0.53	0.23
32	Aomori	0.53	0.38
33	Hokkaido	0.51	0.10
34	Kochi	0.49	0.43
35	Kagawa	0.47	0.77
36	Hyogo	0.42	0.35
37	Fukuoka	0.42	1.12
38	Ehime	0.40	0.15
39	Kanagawa	0.37	−0.58
40	Wakayama	0.31	1.36
41	Hiroshima	0.29	0.53

Rank	Prefecture	Average efficiency score	Change rate of score
42	Mie	0.28	1.83
43	Ibaraki	0.25	−0.26
44	Yamaguchi	0.20	−0.25
45	Chiba	0.15	−0.32
46	Okayama	0.14	0.49
47	Oita	0.13	0.95

Note: The energy efficiency scores in the table are calculated using the estimation results for Model A.

Table 6.
Average energy efficiency scores and change rate of the score.

Rank correlation method	Rank correlation coefficient	P-value
Kendall's tau	−0.2396	0.0175
Spearman	−0.3207	0.0280

Table 7.
Results of rank correlation.

annual rates. These prefectures rank low in average energy efficiency. Therefore, it is highly likely these regions have several electrical machineries and equipment manufacturing units, and their machinery industry has progressive electrification rates, thus contributing to the improvement of energy efficiency. Second, energy efficiency is deteriorating in regions with high energy efficiency levels, including Nara, Tokyo, Yamanashi, Ishikawa, and Saga. This suggests that the regional disparities in energy efficiency are decreasing.

This study verifies the possibility of reducing regional disparities in energy efficiency by calculating the rank correlation coefficient between the average energy efficiency score and its change rate. **Table 7** shows the results of the rank correlation coefficient. The Kendall rank correlation coefficient is −0.2396, which is statistically significant. Spearman's rank correlation coefficient is −0.3207, also being statistically significant. The sign of any rank correlation coefficient is negative, and the improvement in energy efficiency is progressing in the region with a low energy efficiency.

The energy efficiency level is highly related to electrification. **Figure 2** is a cross-sectional plot of the average values for the electrification rate and energy efficiency. The figure clearly illustrates an upward trend. In other words, regions with advanced electrification have high energy efficiency levels. Specifically, regions where offices are concentrated (e.g., Tokyo) are located in the upper right corner, while those with petrochemical complexes (e.g., Oita, Okayama, and Chiba) are in the lower right.

Furthermore, it is also highly possible that energy efficiency improvements have progressed to electrification. **Figure 3** plots the time-series relationship between the electrification rate and energy efficiency and shows an upward trend. In other words, it is highly likely that advanced electrification contributes to energy efficiency improvements. As described above, Mie is likely to report improved energy efficiency, given its progress in electrification. On the other hand, Chiba has lower energy efficiency, given the low energy efficiency of petrochemical complexes.

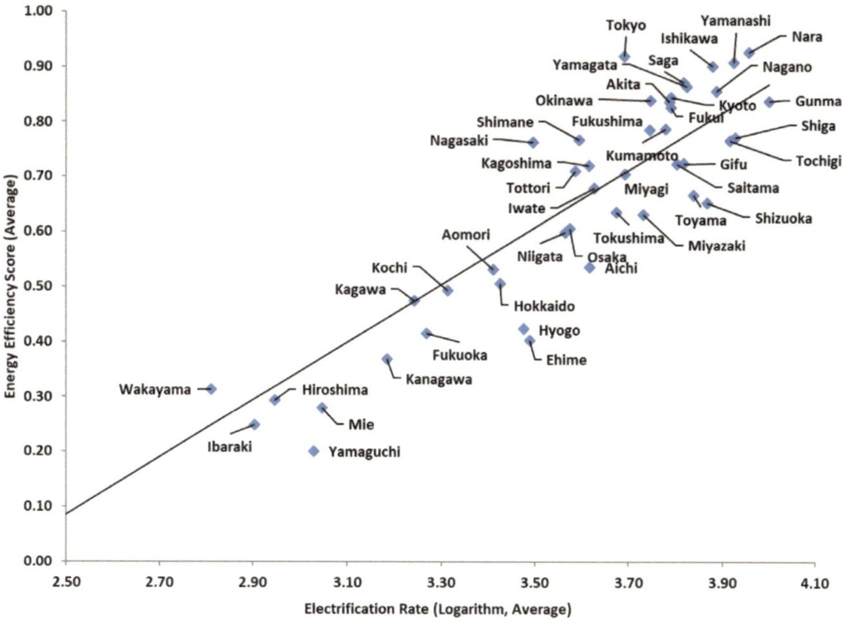

Figure 2.
Static relationship between energy efficiency score and electrification rate.

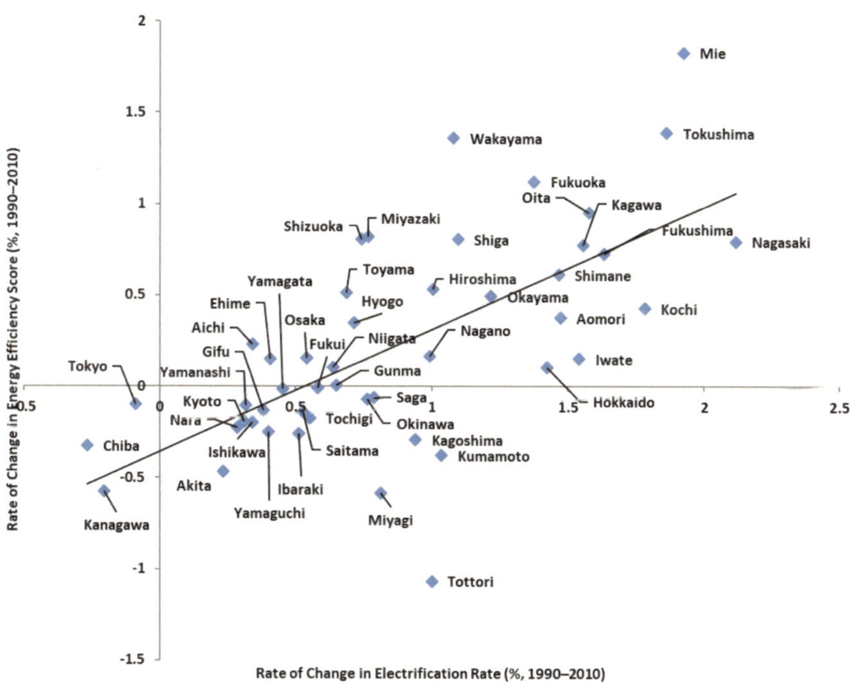

Figure 3.
Dynamic relationship between energy efficiency score and electrification rate.

Finally, this study analyzes the determinants of the electrification rate, which is one of the key factors to improve energy efficiency. **Table 8** presents the estimation results for Eq. (4). First, the F-test checks for fixed effects and rejects the null hypothesis that there is no fixed effect at the 1% significance level. Additionally, the Hausman test rejects the null hypothesis that the fixed effect is a random effect

Method	EF		Panel GMM	
	Coefficient	Standard error	Coefficient	Standard error
Constant (δ)	−0.434**	(0.196)	0.240	(0.264)
δ_{LN}	0.215**	(0.080)	0.331**	(0.084)
δ_{OR}	3.751**	(0.328)	4.781**	(0.368)
δ_{TFP}	0.707**	(0.008)	0.550**	(0.037)
δ_{CDD}	0.001	(0.003)	0.000	(0.003)
δ_{HDD}	0.000	(0.008)	0.001	(0.008)
Number of observations	987		940	
Adjusted R-squared	0.9850		0.9840	
Hausman test	17.086**			
Prob (Hausman)	[0.0043]			
J-statistic			0.0122	
Prob(J-statistic)			[0.9119]	
Instrument			TFP(−1)	

*Note: 1. ** and * indicate significance at the 1 and 5% levels, respectively. 2. The values between parentheses are p-values.*

Table 8.
Panel estimation results on determinants of the electrification rate.

at the 1% significance level. Therefore, the fixed effect model is appropriate for the panel regression analysis. Further, to test the validity of the panel GMM estimation, this study performs a Sargan-Hansen test for the exogeneity of the instrumental variables. From Hansen J's statistical results, the number of instrumental variables is appropriate and satisfies the condition of heteroskedasticity.

The signs for all the variables are consistent under both models. The sign for the establishment size is positive, meaning establishments with a larger number of employees have a higher electrification rate. Further, the higher the proportion of offices, the greater the electrification rate. It is also noteworthy that the sign of an establishment's productivity is positive. This indicates that an increase in the establishment's productivity is proportional to that in the electrification rate. The magnitude of the coefficient on productivity is between 0.475 and 0.676, and it significantly influences the electrification rate. Neither cooling nor heating degree days are statistically significant.

In sum, the establishment scale and productivity are closely related to the electrification rate, which may influence energy efficiency. That is, productivity improves energy efficiency through an increase in electrification at factories and business establishments. Therefore, the efforts to increase the office productivity could improve energy efficiency.

4. Conclusions and policy implications

This study analyzed the energy efficiency levels and their determinants in Japan's industrial sector using an energy demand frontier function. To the best of the author's knowledge, this is the first attempt to do so. Energy intensity has been traditionally used as a proxy for energy efficiency and depends on economic variables such as price and income. However, this study specified energy demand and controlled for price, income, production environment, and climate factors, thus rendering energy efficiency a more accurate index.

This study focused on compact mechanization and electrification as the two main determinants of the improvements in the energy efficiency of the industrial sector. The analysis presented three key findings. First, an installment in large capital facilities deteriorates energy efficiency. Therefore, policies aimed at promoting small- or medium-sized production facility installments lead to improvements in energy efficiency. Second, an increase in the electrification rate of a given region can improve its energy efficiency. Finally, it is necessary to increase the productivity and also the electrification rate, that is, raising the productivity of factories and offices promotes electrification, which considerably contributes to increased energy efficiency. This finding highlights the relationship between increasing productivity and improvements in energy efficiency, suggesting the possibility of the Porter hypothesis being established.

It can be concluded that the energy efficiency of the industrial sector can be improved by developing an appropriately competitive environment and encouraging electrification in each region's energy market. Additionally, electrification increases environmental efficiency by reducing carbon dioxide emissions. Therefore, the promotion of electrification is critical to the achievement of not only energy efficiency but also improving environmental efficiency. Nevertheless, further research is needed to verify whether this trend also applies to other countries to ensure the effectiveness of electrification.

The future research agenda relates to both the micro and macro viewpoints. The former indicates that future studies should examine the energy efficiency of electric power as an energy source from a more diversified viewpoint, including power saving. An important factor that warrants consideration in power consumption efficiency is an appropriate way to account for the efficiency of plant facilities and performance of air conditioning. Since this research could not account for the performance of each device, quantitatively examining this factor warrants further research.

The research agenda from the macro viewpoint clarifies how the increase in urban population density affects energy efficiency, as discussed in Otsuka and Goto [40] and Otsuka [41]. In developed countries, urban compactification is being promoted from the viewpoint of city sustainability. The rise in urban population density exacerbates energy efficiency by causing a heat island phenomenon. Meanwhile, population concentration in cities has the merit of promoting the use of public transportation. Further, cities have more dwelling units than detached houses, and apartments have high thermal insulation and energy efficiency. As such, living in the city center may increase the energy efficiency. It seems that clarifying these problems would deepen the understanding of energy efficiency.

Acknowledgements

This study was funded by the Japan Society for the Promotion of Science (grant no. 18K01614).

Conflict of interest

The author declares no conflict of interest. The funders had no role in the design of the study; the collection, analyses, or interpretation of data; the writing of the manuscript, or the decision to publish the results.

Author details

Akihiro Otsuka
Association of International Arts and Science, Yokohama City University, Yokohama, Japan

*Address all correspondence to: otsuka@yokohama-cu.ac.jp

References

[1] Yang Q, Kaneko S, Fujii H, Yoshida Y. Do exogenous shocks better leverage the benefits of technological change in the staged elimination of differential environmental regulations? Evidence from China's cement industry before and after the 2008 great Sichuan earthquake. Journal of Cleaner Production. 2017;**164**:1167-1179. DOI: 10.1016/j. jclepro. 2017.06.210

[2] Taner T, Sivrioglu M. A techno-economic & cost analysis of a turbine power plant: A case study for sugar plant. Renewable and Sustainable Energy Reviews. 2017;**78**:722-730. DOI: 10.1016/j.rser.2017.04.104

[3] Taner T. Economic analysis of a wind power plant: A case study for the Cappadocia region. Journal of Mechanical Science and Technology. 2018;**32**:1379-1389. DOI: 10.1007/s12206-018-0241-6

[4] Taner T. Energy and exergy analyze of PEM fuel cell: A case study of modeling and simulations. Energy. 2018;**143**:284-294. DOI: 10.1016/j. energy.2017.10.102

[5] Bhattacharyya SC. Energy Economics Concepts, Issues. Markets and Governance. London: Springer-Verlag; 2011

[6] Patterson MG. What is energy efficiency? Concepts, indicators and methodological issues. Energy Policy. 1996;**24**:377-390. DOI: 10.1016/0301-4215(96)00017-1

[7] Energy Information Administration (EIA). Measuring Energy Efficiency in the United States' Economy: A Beginning. US DOE/EIA-0555(95)/2. Washington, DC, USA; 1995

[8] Energy Information Administration (EIA). International Energy Outlook 2013. U.S. Energy Information Administration; 2013

[9] International Energy Agency (IEA). Progress with Implementing Energy Efficiency Policies in the G8. International Energy Agency Paper; 2009

[10] Huntington HG. Been top down so long it looks like bottom up to me. Energy Policy. 1994;**22**:833-838. DOI: 10.1016/0301-4215(94)90142-2

[11] Feijoo ML, Franco JF, Hernández JM. Global warming and the energy efficiency of Spanish industry. Energy Economics. 2002;**24**:405-423. DOI: 10.1016/S0140-9883(02)00013-0

[12] Buck J, Young D. The potential for energy efficiency gains in the Canadian commercial building sector. Energy. 2007;**32**:1769-1780. DOI: 10.1016/j. energy.2006.11.008

[13] Boyd GA. Estimating plant level energy efficiency with a stochastic frontier. Energy Journal. 2008;**29**:23-43. https://www.jstor.org/stable/41323155

[14] Zhou P, Ang BW. Linear programming models for measuring economy-wide energy efficiency performance. Energy Policy. 2008;**36**:2911-2916. DOI: 10.1016/j. enpol.2008.03.041

[15] Filippini M, Hunt LC. Energy demand and energy efficiency in the OECD countries: A stochastic demand frontier approach. Energy Journal. 2011;**32**:59-79. DOI: 10.5547/ISSN0195-6574-EJ-Vol32-No2-3

[16] Filippini M, Hunt LC. US residential energy demand and energy efficiency: A stochastic demand frontier approach. Energy Economics. 2012;**34**:1484-1491. DOI: 10.1016/j. eneco.2012.06.013

[17] Carvalho A. Energy efficiency in transition economies. The Economics of Transition. 2018;**26**:553-578. DOI: 10.1111/ecot.12152

[18] Aranda-Uson A, Ferreira G, Mainar-Toledo MD, Scarpellini S, Liera E. Energy consumption analysis of Spanish food and drink, textile, chemical and non-metallic mineral products sectors. Energy. 2012;**42**:477-485. DOI: 10.1016/j.energy.2012.03.021

[19] Lin B, Yang LS. The potential estimation and factor analysis of China's energy conservation on thermal power industry. Energy Policy. 2013;**62**:354-362. DOI: 10.1016/j.enpol.2013.07.079

[20] Lin B, Wang X. Exploring energy efficiency in China's iron and steel industry: A stochastic frontier approach. Energy Policy. 2014;**72**:87-96. DOI: 10.1016/j.enpol.2014.04.043

[21] Lin B, Long HA. Stochastic frontier analysis of energy efficiency of China's chemical industry. Journal of Cleaner Production. 2015;**87**:235-244. DOI: 10.1016/j.jclepro.2014.08.104

[22] Lin BQ, Du KR. Technology gap and China's regional energy efficiency: A parametric meta frontier approach. Energy Economics. 2013;**40**:529-536. DOI: 10.1016/j.eneco.2013.08.013

[23] Filippini M, Lin B. Estimation of the energy efficiency in Chinese provinces. Energy Efficiency. 2016;**9**:1315-1328. DOI: 10.1007/s12053-016-9425-z

[24] Zhou P, Ang BW, Zhou DQ. Measuring economy-wide energy efficiency performance: A parametric frontier approach. Applied Energy. 2012;**90**:196-200. DOI: 10.1016/j.apenergy.2011.02.025

[25] Otsuka A. Determinants of efficiency in residential electricity demand. Evidence from Japan. Energy, Sustainability and Society. 2017;**7**:1-10. DOI: 10.1186/s13705-017-0135-y

[26] Otsuka A. Regional determinants of energy efficiency: Residential energy demand in Japan. Energies. 2018;**11**: 1-14. DOI: 10.3390/en11061557

[27] Porter ME, Van der Linde C. Toward a new conception of the environment competitiveness relationship. Journal of Economic Perspectives. 1995;**9**:97-118. https://www.jstor.org/stable/2138392

[28] Boyd GA, Pang JX. Estimating the linkage between energy efficiency and productivity. Energy Policy. 2000;**28**:289-296. DOI: 10.1016/S0301-4215(00)00016-1

[29] Otsuka A, Goto M, Sueyoshi T. Energy efficiency and agglomeration economies: The case of Japanese manufacturing industries. Regional Science Policy and Practice. 2014;**6**: 195-212. DOI: 10.1111/rsp3.12039

[30] Thompson P, Taylor TG. The capital-energy substitutability debate. The Review of Economics and Statistics. 1995;**77**:565-569. https://www.jstor.org/stable/2109916

[31] Metcalf GE, Hassett KA. Measuring the energy savings from home improvement investment: Evidence from monthly billing data. The Review of Economics and Statistics. 1999;**81**:516-528. https://www.jstor.org/stable/2646774

[32] Reiss PC, White MW. What changes energy consumption? Prices and public pressures. RAND Journal of Economics. 2008;**39**:636-663. https://www.jstor.org/stable/25474390

[33] Otsuka A, Goto M. Estimation and determinants of energy efficiency in Japanese regional economies. Regional Science Policy and Practice. 2015;**7**: 89-101. DOI: 10.1111/rsp3.12058

[34] Aigner DJ, Lovell CAK, Schmidt P. Formulation and estimation of stochastic frontier production function model. Journal of Econometrics. 1977;**6**:21-37. DOI: 10.1016/0304-4076(77)90052-5

[35] Battese GE, Coelli TJA. A model for technical inefficiency effects in a stochastic frontier production function for panel data. Empirical Economics. 1995;**20**:325-332. DOI: 10.1007/BF01205442

[36] Coelli TJ. Recent development in frontier modeling and efficiency measurement. Australian Journal of Agricultural Economics. 1995;**39**:219-245. DOI: 10.1111/j.1467-8489.1995.tb00552.x

[37] Jondrow J, Knox Lovell CA, Materov IS, Schmidt P. On the estimation of technical inefficiency in the stochastic frontier production function model. Journal of Economics. 1982;**19**:233-238. DOI: 10.1016/0304-4076(82)90004-5

[38] Otsuka A. Regional Energy Demand and Energy Efficiency in Japan. Switzerland: Springer; 2017. DOI: 10.1007/978-3-319-47566-0

[39] Otsuka A, Goto M. Total factor productivity and the convergence of disparities in Japanese regions. The Annals of Regional Science. 2016;**56**:419-432. DOI: 10.1007/s00168-016-0745-x

[40] Otsuka A, Goto M. Regional determinants of energy intensity in Japan: The impact of population density. Asia-Pacific Journal of Regional Science. 2018;**2**:257-278. DOI: 10.1007/s41685-017-0045-1

[41] Otsuka A. Population agglomeration and residential energy consumption: Evidence from Japan. Sustainability. 2018;**10**:1-12. DOI: 10.3390/su10020469

Chapter 6

Nuclear Energy Policy after the Fukushima Nuclear Accident: An Analysis of "Polarized Debate" in Japan

Tatsujiro Suzuki

Abstract

The Tokyo Electric Power's Fukushima Daiichi nuclear accident in 2011 was a turning point for Japan's nuclear energy and overall energy policy. In reality, Japan has reduced its dependence on nuclear energy drastically despite the government's policy to maintain nuclear energy as a major power source. Even with sharp drop in production from nuclear energy, Japan could achieve carbon reduction of around 60–70% by 2050 even without nuclear power. But the biggest impact of the Fukushima accident is the loss of public trust. The policy debate on nuclear energy is now divided between "pro" and "anti" of nuclear power. The aim of this study is to analyze why such "polarized debate" has not been resolved and find a way to restore public trust. This study analyzes three important nuclear energy policy issues, i.e., decommissioning of Fukushima Daiichi nuclear plant, spent nuclear fuel and waste management, and plutonium stockpile management. The analysis of these three cases suggest that lack of independent oversight organizations is a common cause of impasse of nuclear energy policy debate. The author argues that Japan needs to establish independent oversight organizations in order to gain public trust and solve important policy issues regardless of the future of nuclear energy.

Keywords: Fukushima accident, polarized debate, public trust, independent oversight, nuclear waste, plutonium

1. Introduction

The Tokyo Electric Power Fukushima Daiichi nuclear accident was a turning point for Japan's nuclear energy and overall energy policy.

The biggest impact is the huge drop in the number of reactors operating and its share in electricity supply in Japan. Before the Fukushima accident in 2010, the share of nuclear energy was about 25%, and it went down to zero in 2012 and still only 1.7% in 2016 [1]. It is surprising that despite such sharp reduction in nuclear power generation, no serious power shortage has happened in Japan. One of the main reasons is sharp reduction in electricity consumption and peak demand. In FY 2011, power consumption dropped about 3.8% from FY 2010, and consumption continued to decline until FY 2016 and is now about 10% below the level of FY 2010. Peak demand also declined sharply. Its peak demand in FY 2010 was 178 GWe

IntechOpen

in August 23, 2010 but declined to 153 GW in FY 2015 on August 7, 2015, which is about 14% reduction [1].

Another major impact of the Fukushima accident is loss of public trust and dramatic shift in public opinion on nuclear power. Before the Fukushima accident, majority of the public was in favor of either maintaining or expansion of nuclear power, but now majority of the public was in favor of either immediate shutdown of all reactors or gradual phaseout of nuclear power. Based on such shift in public opinion, the government under the Democratic Party of Japan in 2012 issued a new energy policy to phase out nuclear power by the end of 2030 [2]. But the new government under the Liberal Democratic Party reversed its policy and still maintains nuclear power as an important power source [3]. But loss of public trust has not been restored, and majority of the public still believes that severe nuclear accident could happen despite the new and much tougher nuclear safety regulation standards and establishment by the newly established, independent Nuclear Regulation Authority (NRA) in 2013.

As a result, whenever a reactor is ready for restart up, public debate occurs and legal cases follow although the pronuclear government and utility industry insist that restart-up of nuclear power is necessary for economy and energy security. In short, the country is now divided into "pro" and "anti" nuclear energy, and policy debate is often polarized and has led to unproductive discussion, and major policy issues remain unsolved. It is important to clarify the issues that need to be addressed regardless of the future of nuclear energy. By focusing on these issues and through more productive policy discussion, consensus may emerge among the public on what to do to solve those important issues.

Meanwhile, new energy policy of Japan should reflect new developments in renewable energy and energy efficiency in which the public has strong support. Given structural change in energy demand and rapid development of renewable energy, Japan could reduce its carbon emission by 60–70% by 2050, based on the recent analysis [4, 5].

The aim of this study is to analyze why "polarized debate" has not been resolved and find a way to restore public trust by focusing on issues that need to be resolved regardless of the future of nuclear energy.

2. Loss of public trust

The loss of public trust is one of the biggest impacts of the Fukushima nuclear accident. Public opinion on nuclear power in Japan has changed dramatically since the Fukushima accident.

According to the public polling done by Japan Atomic Energy Relations Organization [6], the ratio of public who believe that nuclear power is necessary was 35.4% in 2010 but dropped to 23.5% in 2011 after the accident and further dropped to 17.9% in 2017. At the same time, the ratio of the public who do not trust nuclear power (community) jumped from 10.2% in 2010 to 24.3% in 2011 and now even increased to 30.2% in 2017.

The public has lost faith in nuclear safety regulation too. Faith has not been fully restored even after a new independent Nuclear Regulation Authority was established in 2012, and new, much tougher regulatory standards were introduced. According to the same JAERO study, the ratio of the public who trust the government and nuclear industry is 1.9 and 1.2%, respectively, and the ratio of the public who do not trust the government and nuclear industry is 20.5 and 22.0%, respectively. The reasons for "not trustworthy" cited by those are lack of information disclosure (nuclear industry 68.3%, government 62.5%), insufficient preparation and management on safety (nuclear industry 60.4%, government 54.1%), and not speaking honestly (nuclear industry 59.8%, government 59.2%). As a result, the ratio of the public who think that nuclear power should be increased and/or maintained before the Fukushima accident continuously dropped to 10.1% in 2014 and only 6.9% in 2017. On the other hand, the ratio of the public who are in favor of phasing out and/or should be abolished now increased to 79.6% in 2017 from 56.2% in 2013.

In the latest polling undertaken by Mainichi Shimbun in March 2018 [7], the proportion of the public who oppose the restarting of existing reactors rose to 55%, an increase of 2% points from previous polling on this question. And the proportion of the public who support the restarting of existing reactors was down to 26%, a decline of 4% from the previous polling. As a result, its gap between the opposition and the support became bigger.

The previous government under the Democratic Party of Japan tried to restore public trust by introducing more open decision-making process. Prime Minister Naoto Kan announced that it would critically review nuclear energy policy "from scratch" and set up new policy-making process to encourage "national public debate" on nuclear energy. It set up a new cabinet-level Council on Energy and Environment and promoted public participation in policy-making process. As a result, a new "Innovative Energy and Environmental Strategy" was issued in September 2012, incorporating results of public opinion polls which showed that majority of the public was in favor of "phasing out nuclear power." The new strategy aimed at phasing out nuclear power by the end of the 2030s and did not allow for new construction of nuclear power plants [2].

But newly elected Shinzo Abe's government abolished the previous government's "nuclear phaseout" policy and abolished the open policy-making process to reflect public opinions to the decision-making. On April 11, 2014, the new Strategic Energy Plan was adopted by the cabinet [3]. Although the new plan stated that Japan will reduce its dependence on nuclear energy as much as possible, it still maintains that nuclear power is an important "base-load power source" (i.e., essential power source which should be operated 24 hours/day without changing its output). As a result, its "dual policy goals" (the goal of "decreasing dependence on nuclear power as much as possible" and the goal of "using nuclear power as a base-load power source") send confusing signals to the public and energy market. Later the METI published its future energy mix projection, suggesting that nuclear power's share in 2030 should be around 20–22% [8]. In order to achieve that goal, not only existing reactors should be restarted, but Japan may need new reactors replacing old reactors. Since then, the debate over nuclear energy—especially the restart of existing reactors—has been polarized as the government pushed its pronuclear stance, while the public was still in favor of eventual phaseout of nuclear energy.

On July 3, 2018, the Japanese government adopted METI's new "Strategic Energy Plan" as a cabinet decision [9]. The new Strategic Energy Plan has some new features compared with the previous 2014 plan, such as stronger emphasis on renewable energy and new statement on plutonium stockpile which will be discussed later in this paper. But in overall, the plan is not so different from the previous plan. The plan still defines nuclear power as an important base-load power, while it aims to reduce its dependency on nuclear power as much as possible as was the case in the previous strategic plan in 2014.

Although the majority of the public seems to be in favor of phasing out nuclear energy, the Japanese government continues to maintain its commitment to nuclear power. As of October 26, 2018, only 9 out of 39 existing reactors are operating, while 6 received operating licenses but have not yet started operation, and 16 reactors have been closed (to be decommissioned) since the accident. But still there are 14 reactors that have not applied for re-license, while 3 reactors are under construction [10]. It is not certain when and whether those reactors will receive operating licenses in the near future.

Political process to restart the nuclear reactors is complex and not straightforward in Japan. Technically, getting the approval from the NRA is sufficient to start up the reactor, but not politically sufficient. Utilities must get local governments' approval under the so-called Safety Agreement, which is a gentlemen agreement (not legally binding) between local governments and utilities. In particular, evacuation issue is the major hurdle for restart up, as evacuation plan is not a subject of NRA licensing process, and thus it is not clear how and who determines the appropriateness of evacuation plans.

Another challenge is legal lawsuits against utilities and/or government on nuclear safety. After the Fukushima accident, it is no longer automatic to assume that local residents and nuclear opponents lose the case. Uncertainties about legal decisions on nuclear safety issues are increasing due to different interpretation of "safety" by the courts. For example, on December 13, 2017, the high court in Hiroshima granted the injunction requested by the residents in Hiroshima and opponents for the operating Ikata #3 and #4 reactors. This was the first time that the high court granted the injunction against operating reactors [11]. However, on September 25, 2018, the same high court in Hiroshima now granted the objections from Shikoku Denryoku who is the operator of Ikata reactors and allowed the utility to restart the reactor. It turned out the judges who made the decision to grant the utilities are different from those who made decision to grant the injunction in 2017 [12].

3. Impact on energy policy of the Fukushima accident and long-term prospects on carbon emissions

As noted above, Japan's energy supply and demand picture has dramatically changed after the Fukushima nuclear accident. The sudden reduction of power production from nuclear power forced Japan to increase in fossil fuel consumption which led to increase in electricity rates, from 20 yen/kWh (the average of consumer electricity rate) in 2010 to more than 25 yen/kWh in 2014. But then, due to decrease in fossil fuel prices, it went down to about 20 yen/kWh in 2015 [1]. Increased consumption of fossil fuel resulted in increase of CO_2 emission of Japan, peaking its emission at 1.4 billion tons in 2013, but then declined to 1.3 billion tons in 2015 and 2016. The reasons for decline of CO_2 emission are increasing production of renewable energy and increased energy efficiency which led to reduction of energy consumption itself [13].

The energy efficiency improvement rate was almost equal to the one achieved after the first oil crisis in 1973. The average improvement rate of energy efficiency was 2.9% per from FY 1973 to 1985, while it was 3.2% per year from FY 2011 to 2014 [4].

According to a study done by a team at Japan Center for Economic Research (JCER) [4, 5], such trends will likely to continue based on the assumption that fossil fuel price will continue to increase and Japan's energy and economic structure will shift to more energy efficient nonmanufacturing industries. Furthermore, the study assumes expansion of renewable energy up to 60% of total electricity production through interviews of experts of renewable energy in Japan. The study also assumes that 15% of electricity production will come from nuclear power from 2030, which may require construction of new reactors to replace old reactors in Japan.

Based on such assumptions, Japan could reduce CO_2 emissions by 60% by 2030 or even 70% with introduction of environmental tax. Nuclear power, if it is too expensive, could be replaced by carbon capture storage (CCS) fossil power plants which are assumed to be commercially competitive by 2030. In fact, the study also analyzes the impact of the Fukushima accident on the economics of nuclear power. Due to increase in accident associate costs, nuclear power's commercial competitive advantage may disappear, and thus total cost of carbon reduction strategy without nuclear may not be so expensive compared with the one with nuclear power [4].

The study results suggest that Japan's carbon reduction strategy may not need nuclear power as was expected before. In short, the most important factor in carbon reduction strategy is likely to be energy efficiency improvement and expansion of renewable energy, and thus dependence on nuclear power can be reduced as much as possible. In fact, public trust is essential in solving key policy issues regardless of the future of nuclear energy.

4. Analysis of three issues which need to be resolved regardless of the future of nuclear energy

Primarily due to loss of public trust, polarized debate has not led to constructive policy debate to solve important policy issues that need to be addressed regardless of the future of nuclear power. What would be necessary to avoid polarized debate and constructive discussion which could lead to solutions to important policy issues? This section deals with three important policy issues and examines the ways to overcome the current difficulties of polarized debate.

4.1 The decommissioning of the Fukushima Daiichi reactors

More than 7 years have passed since the earthquake, but the accident is not completely over. About 60,000 evacuated residents in Fukushima are still living in temporary housing and are still uncertain as to when and whether they can return to their original hometowns. Although conditions at the Fukushima power stations have improved, it will take more than at least 40 years to decommission the plant, but the removal of melted debris is the most challenging task with high risk. It is still not clear whether the debris can be removed safely and how to dispose all radioactive wastes from the decommissioning.

The task of decommissioning of the Fukushima Daiichi reactors is obviously the most challenging task that the global nuclear industry has faced. The Tokyo Electric Power Co (TEPCO) is still responsible for managing this important and challenging task, but the government has helped TEPCO by setting up the Inter-Ministerial Council for Contaminated Water and Decommissioning Issues which publish the "Mid-and-Long-Term Roadmap towards the Decommissioning of TEPCO's Fukushima Daiichi Nuclear Power Station". The most recent one, published on September 26, 2017, again delayed the first phase (removing the spent fuel from storage pools of units 1–3) for more than 3 years [14].

There have been concerns about lack of transparency and independent oversight on the whole decommissioning process. The Japan Atomic Energy Commission, which is an advisory organ under the cabinet office, recommended that the government should establish an independent (third party) organization with overseas experts as members to assess and audit the entire measures in order to maximize transparency [15]. But such independent organization has not been established by the government.

After Prime Minister made a speech at the 125th Session of the International Olympic Committee (IOC) on September 7, 2013 [16], in which he stressed that the situation in Fukushima is "under control," the government announced that it would take more responsibility in contaminated water problems. The government set up "Inter-Ministerial Council for Contaminated Water and Decommissioning Issues," and "frozen wall method" was chosen by the Council as the best technology to deal with the contaminated water. However, it was not clear why this technology was chosen. Many underground water experts raise doubts about the effectiveness of the technology which is often used for a small-scale underground water treatment but has never been used for such a large-scale operation. Experts suggested that there are simpler and cheaper alternative technologies available, but selection was made in a closed meeting without full disclosure of its selection process [17]. The frozen wall was completed, but NRA gave a license to start operation of the wall on August 15, 2017, but its effectiveness is still unclear.

The second example of lack of transparency is the estimate of total cost of decommissioning. On December 20, 2016, the Committee for Reforming TEPCO and Overcoming 1F Challenges under the METI published new cost estimate for decommissioning of Fukushima Daiichi and compensation and decontamination of land. The total cost jumped from previous estimate of 11 trillion yen to 22 trillion yen [18]. But the foundations of such estimate are very weak. The analysis done by an independent economic think tank, Japan Center for Economic Research (JCER), did its own cost estimate, and it would be between 50 and 70 trillion yen [19]. JCER suggested that METI's estimates do not include final disposal cost of the waste coming from the decommissioning and decontamination which METI admitted. But based on the TEPCO Committee's estimate, METI made a decision that part of the total cost will be paid by other power producers and taxpayers.

According to the recent report published at the public hearing organized by the subcommittee on treatment of contaminated water on August 30, 2018, cumulative radioactivity in tank storage is now reaching to 1000 tera Becquerel (TBq), and the number of storage tank is now 860 units [20]. It is suggested by TEPCO that there will be no enough space to build additional storage tanks by 2020.

The subcommittee presented recommended that the water, which still contains tritium but no other radioactive materials which will be removed by the processing facilities (called "ALPS"), be released to the sea after confirming that the radioactive concentration is below the standard agreed beforehand, which is 1500 Bq/l. This standard is extremely low compared with drinking water standard of tritium water set by the World Health Organization (WHO) which is 10,000 Bq/l. But one of the conditions to release the tritium water is that all other radioactive substances are removed by the ALPS below detectable limit or regulatory standards. Unfortunately, it was reported that some radioactive materials such as strontium-90 (Sr-90) were not completely removed and its concentration was above the regulatory standards [21].

It would be fair to conclude that if there is an independent oversight organization, all above cases could have been avoided, or at least the public trust might have been better by presenting objective assessment of the situation.

4.2 Spent fuel and radioactive waste management

Even before the Fukushima accident, what to do with accumulating spent fuel on-site at nuclear power plants was a major policy issue for nuclear utilities and the government. The basic policy for spent fuel management in Japan has been (and still is) "reprocessing and recycling plutonium" for energy use. As a result, in Japan, spent fuel is considered as "resource (asset)" and not as a "waste." Under the Japanese Law on Final Disposal of Specified Radioactive Waste (which is the law for geological disposal of radioactive waste), the "specified waste" is defined as the waste coming out of reprocessing plant, i.e., vitrified waste and TRU waste, but spent fuel is not included. Like many other countries, Japan has not found a final repository site for high-level radioactive waste (HLW).

In Japan, the Law on Final Disposal of Specified Radioactive Waste was passed in 2000 which established Nuclear Waste Management Organization (NUMO) as the principal implementation institution for final disposal. But no single site has been found even for literature survey which is the first step of siting of disposal site. Since then, only one town (Toyo Town) volunteered to be a candidate for site survey but later canceled the request due to strong public opposition. In order to improve public acceptance, in 2010, JAEC issued a request to the Science Council of Japan for their advice on how to improve public communication on HLW. This was the first time that JAEC issued a request to an independent third party to review its program. The Science Council of Japan (SCJ) recommended "fundamental reform" of Japan's HLW waste disposal policy. In particular, one important recommendation was to secure an open discussion forum where "independent, autonomous scientific groups can exchange their opinions" [22].

The JAEC responded with its own policy statement on December 18, 2012 [23]. JAEC agreed with SCJ on above point and recommended that the government "establish an independent and functionally effective third party organization to provide suitable advice to the government and related parties in time."

Responding to SCJ and JAEC's recommendation, METI set up two working groups, one of which is to look at the siting process including public participation. That working group also recommended that the government should "set up a scheme to conduct independent from a third party's point of view" [24]. Based on its findings, the Japanese government published its new basic policy for HLW Disposal in May 2015 which specifies that JAEC is the organization to review the METI's program as an independent organization [25]. But JAEC is not truly an independent organization as it is responsible for promoting nuclear energy under the basic Atomic Energy Act.

The following incident proved that current scheme is still lacking such independent review function. NUMO initiated public consultation process based on this map, but the NUMO again lost its public trust in this public consultation process. It was reported that NUMO's contracted organization paid students and others to attend the public consultation meetings so that the meetings seemed successful in gathering general public [26].

Again, one fundamental issue is public trust. The Science Council of Japan recently published a report to follow up its own report published in 2013. In the new report, they re-emphasized the importance of a "consensus building process" for HLW disposal and proposed the creation of "national people's conference on radioactive waste" [27].

4.3 Plutonium stockpile management

As noted above, Japan's basic policy is to reprocess all spent fuel and recover plutonium and uranium to recycle them for energy use. However, in reality, the plutonium usage program (recycling as mixed-oxide (MOX) fuel into existing reactors and fast breeder reactors in the future) has been delayed significantly. As a result, as of the end of 2017, Japan possessed about 47.3 tons of separated plutonium (10.5 tons in Japan and 36.7 tons in France and the United Kingdom where Japan had commercial reprocessing contracts) (**Table 1**) [28]. This is the largest stockpile among nonnuclear weapon states and could increase further if the Rokkasho reprocessing plant starts operation in 2021 and its recycling program into 16–18 reactors as currently planned does not smoothly move ahead [29].

This plutonium stockpile issue has raised international concern. In 2016, a former US government official expressed his concern over Japan's plutonium stockpile and its reprocessing policy. Jon Wolfsthal, Senior Director for Arms Control and Nonproliferation at the National Security Council said the following in a recent interview with Kyodo Press:

> *"There is no question that plutonium recycling in Japan has been expensive. That is a challenging future for Japan. If Japan were to change course, they would find the United States to be supportive.... The upcoming renewal in 2018 of a bilateral nuclear agreement with Japan has the potential to become a very controversial issue...If Japan keeps recycling plutonium, what is to stop other countries from thinking the exact same thing?"* [30].

As noted above, under the 1988 US-Japan bilateral nuclear energy cooperation agreement, Japan has been given a 30-year "programmatic prior consent" on reprocessing, i.e., unlike a typical bilateral agreement, Japan does not need a case-by-case prior consent on reprocessing. This has been considered as a "special privilege" as only the European Atomic Energy Community (EURATOM) and Japan are given such special arrangements. The 1988 agreement was extended without any amendment in July 2018, but now the agreement could be canceled if either party notifies the other party 6 months in advance.

Concern over reprocessing programs are also spreading in Northeast Asia. The ROK government, during bilateral negotiation with the USA, strongly insisted that it has a sovereign right to reprocessing as Japan does. China is now planning to build a commercial reprocessing plant, imported from France, while criticizing Japan for holding a large plutonium stockpile. So, it has become a regional security issue and needs to be addressed with serious attention [31].

In order to reduce such international concern, the METI's new Energy Strategic Plan [5] mentions for the first time that Japan aims to "reduce its plutonium stockpile". In addition, on July 31, 2018, JAEC also published its new "Basic Principles on Japan's Utilization of Plutonium," which says the following:

	2016 (kg)	2017 (kg)
Stock in Japan (Pu total)		
Reprocessing plants	3913	3863
MOX fuel plant	3805	3854
Stored at reactors	2126	2829
Subtotal (Pu fissile)*	9844 (6605)	10,548 (7050)
Stocks in Europe (Pu total)		
The United Kingdom	20,839	21,232
France	16,217	15,486
Subtotal: Pu total (Pu fissile)	37,058 (24,510)	36,718 (24,265)
Total (Pu fissile)	46,902 (31,115)	47,266 (31,315)

**Fissile plutonium (Pu 239 and Pu 241) contents of plutonium which is typically about 60% of total plutonium which includes non-fissile isotope of plutonium (Pu 240 and Pu 242).*
Source: [23].

Table 1.
Japan's plutonium stockpile (as of the end of 2016 and 2017).

Japan will reduce the size of plutonium stockpile. Based upon realization of the following measures, the stockpile is not to increase from the current level. [32].

Although such new policy can be a positive step, that may not be enough. In 2017, strong policy recommendations were made by experts from the USA and Japan who participated in an International Conference on Plutonium Policy (PuPo 2017). They recommend to establish a "Joint Commission" between the US and Japanese governments to review the issue of nuclear fuel cycle policy and to analyze ways to deal with plutonium stockpile owned by both the Japanese and US governments [33]. In fact, experts from both inside and outside of Japan recently recommended to revise Japan's nuclear fuel cycle policy and to find specific ways to reduce plutonium stockpile [34, 35].

While all recommendations would be helpful, the recommendation by the International Conference (PuPo 2017) is particularly interesting. The participants acknowledge the importance of "independent oversight" and recommend to establish "US-Japan bilateral joint commission" which can play such role.

5. Results and discussion: lack of independent oversight is the common problem

As can be seen from the above three cases, Japan's policy debate is now polarized between "pro" and "anti" which led to unconstructive policy debate over important policy issues which need to be resolved regardless of the future of nuclear power. It is the lack of independent oversight that needs to be addressed.

In the first case of decommissioning process of the Fukushima Daiichi reactor, lack of independent oversight resulted in wrong choice of technology dealing with contaminated water and inappropriate treatment of contaminated water. In the second case of disposal of radioactive waste, despite recommendations within the government, the METI has not established an independent oversight organization. Instead it still relies on JAEC which is not truly an independent organization. This led to lack of public trust and misconduct by NUMO. The third case dealing with plutonium stockpile also shows that independent oversight organization is recommended to solve complex technical/social and even international security issues involved.

In fact, right after the Fukushima accident, JAEC emphasized in its policy statements that having an independent oversight by the third party is essential to restore public trust and more constructive policy debate. The proposal to establish such an independent oversight organization was made in the context of (1) decommissioning process of the Fukushima Daiichi reactors, (2) decision-making process of final disposal of radioactive waste, and (3) assessment of nuclear fuel cycle and R&D programs. In all these cases, the assessment has been done only by the government agencies or the advisory council under the responsible government agencies.

What constitutes the key characteristics of "independent, third" party for the oversight process? The author argues that the following four conditions are essential:

First, independent funding and secretariat; it is essential that the organization must have independent funding and its own secretariat. In fact, JAEC was criticized in 2012 that its secretariat staff came from power companies and nuclear industry. Later, JAEC released those staff to be more independent. Still their staff come from other government agencies and it has no own staff.

Second, independent expertise; unless the organization has its own independent expertise, it has to rely on the outside organizations. Their analysis and judgment may not be independent if it does not have enough expertise in the organization.

Third, legal authority; independency must be institutionalized by legal status, and clear statute is needed. Ambiguous status of the organization can lose its influence and effectiveness.

Finally, complete transparency in its decision-making process. It is essential that transparency must be institutionalized backed by legal standard so that it can be verified later.

The establishment of independent oversight organization is also recommended by the National Diet of Japan Fukushima Nuclear Accident Independent Investigation Commission in 2012. In its recommendation 7, it says the following:

> *"A system for appointing independent investigation committees, including experts largely from the private sector, must be developed to deal with unresolved issues, including, but not limited to, the decommissioning process of reactors, dealing with spent fuel issues, limiting accident effects and decontamination" [36].*

In May 2017, the Diet finally established an advisory board, consisting of eight independent experts but has not established the independent investigating committees recommended above even 7 years after the accident. If the government cannot establish such independent oversight organization, the Diet can set up such independent organization to overcome Japan's polarized policy debate over nuclear power.

6. Conclusions

The Fukushima nuclear accident has not been over yet. The impacts of the Fukushima accident continue and have changed the nature of energy policy debate dramatically. The accident also triggered the changes of energy supply/demand structure significantly. The following are the main conclusions of this study:

1. Despite large reduction of nuclear energy production, Japan has managed to keep supply/demand in balance and reduced both electricity rate and carbon emissions primarily due to reduction in power consumption through improved energy efficiency.

2. Such trends are likely to continue if fossil fuel prices continue to rise and Japan could reduce its carbon emission more than 60% by 2050, with or without nuclear power.

3. The loss of public trust is one of the most important impacts of the Fukushima accident, and the majority of the public is now in favor of phasing out of nuclear power eventually. Still the Japanese government maintains that nuclear power is an important energy source and has not changed basic nuclear energy policy. As a result, nuclear policy debate in Japan has been polarized.

4. Based on three important policy case studies, it is found that lack of independent oversight can be a common cause for blocking the constructive debate leading to ways to solve important policy issues.

5. Establishment of such independent oversight organization has been recommended by both within and outside of the government, but it has not been realized. In order to overcome polarized policy debate, either the government or the Diet needs to establish such independent oversight organization.

Acknowledgements

The author acknowledges valuable financial assistance given by Japan Center for Economic Research and the Research Center for Nuclear Weapons Abolition, Nagasaki University (RECNA), and invaluable advice/comments from Prof. Tadahiro Katsuta and Mr. Tomoyoshi Hirata of Meiji University.

Conflict of interest

The author has no conflict of interest as no funding was given to the author by the nuclear industry or any other stakeholder organizations.

Author details

Tatsujiro Suzuki
Research Center for Nuclear Weapons Abolition, Nagasaki University (RECNA), Nagasaki, Japan

*Address all correspondence to: suzukitatu@nagasaki-u.ac.jp

References

[1] Ministry of Economy, Trade and Industry (METI), Enerugi Hakusho 2018 (White Paper on Energy 2018) (in Japanese). 2018. Available from: http://www.enecho.meti.go.jp/about/whitepaper/2018html/2-1-4.html

[2] Council on Energy and Environment, Cabinet Office. Innovative Energy and Environmental Strategy (in Japanese). 2012. Available from: http://www.cas.go.jp/jp/seisaku/npu/policy09/pdf/20120914/20120914_1.pdf

[3] Ministry of Economy, Trade and Industry. Strategic Energy Plan (provisional translation). 2014. Available from: http://www.enecho.meti.go.jp/en/category/others/basic_plan/pdf/4th_strategic_energy_plan.pdf

[4] Suzuki T, Kobayashi T, Kobayashi H, Iwata K. Aiming at a low carbon society in Japan by 2050: Impact of the Fukushima nuclear accident and CO_2 reduction target. Economics of Energy & Environmental Policy. 2016;5(1):89-103

[5] Iwata K, Kobayashi H, Suzuki T, Kobayashi T. Kankyo-zei Donyu de CO_2 2050 Nen ni 7wari Sakugen Kano (70% CO_2 reduction by 2050 is possible through introduction of environmental tax) (in Japanese). 2017. Available from: https://www.jcer.or.jp/jcer_download_log.php?post_id=26333&file_post_id=29798

[6] Japan Atomic Energy Relations Organization (JAERO). Genshiryoku ni kannsuru Seron Chosa (Public Opinion Survey on Nuclear Energy Utilization). 2018. Available from: http://www.jaero.or.jp/data/01jigyou/tyousakenkyu29.html

[7] Shimbun M, Saikado G. Hantai 55%, Sansei 26%, Sa Kakudai (Public Opinion Survey on Re-startup of Nuclear Power Plants, not in favor 55%, Favor 26%, the Gap widens). 2018. Available from: https://mainichi.jp/articles/20170313/k00/00m/010/101000c

[8] Ministry of Economy, Trade and Industry (METI). Japan's Energy Plan. 2015. Available from: http://www.enecho.meti.go.jp/en/category/brochures/pdf/energy_plan_2015.pdf

[9] Ministry of Economy, Trade and Industry (METI). Strategic Energy Plan (provisional translation). 2018. Available from: http://www.enecho.meti.go.jp/en/category/others/basic_plan/5th/pdf/strategic_energy_plan.pdf

[10] Japan Nuclear Safety Institute. Licensing Status for the Japanese nuclear facilities. 2018. Available from: http://www.genanshin.jp/english/facility/map/index.html

[11] Shimbun M. Ikata Genpatsu, Unten Sashitome, Kosai reberu, hatsu handan (Injunction on Ikata Nuclear Power plant, first decision ever by the high court) (in Japanese). 2017. Available from: https://mainichi.jp/articles/20171213/k00/00e/040/311000c

[12] Shimbun A. Ikata Genpatsu no Saikado, Kousai Ga Yonin, Sashitome Sosho Karishobun Torikeshi (High Court Reversed its Injunction Decision to Allow Ikata Reactors to Operate) (in Japanese). 2018. Available from: https://digital.asahi.com/articles/ASL9M4FHKL9MPITB00P.html

[13] Ministry of Environment. Japan's National Greenhouse Gas Emissions in Fiscal Year 2016. 2018. Available from: https://www.env.go.jp/en/headline/2368.html

[14] Inter-Ministerial Council for Contaminated Water and Decommissioning Issues. Mid-and-Long-Term Roadmap towards the Decommissioning of TEPCO's

Fukushima Daiichi Nuclear Power Station. 2017. Available from: http://www.meti.go.jp/english/earthquake/nuclear/decommissioning/pdf/20170926_01a.pdf

[15] Japan Atomic Energy Commission. Progress of Medium-and Long-term Efforts to Decommissioning Fukushima Dai-ichi Nuclear Power Plant (NPP) of TEPCO (statement). 2012. Available from: http://www.aec.go.jp/jicst/NC/about/kettei/121127-1_e.pdf

[16] Prime Minister's Office. Presentation by Prime Minister Shinzo Abe at the 125th Session of the International Olympic Committee (IOC). 2013. Available from: https://japan.kantei.go.jp/96_abe/statement/201309/07ioc_presentation_e.html

[17] Nihon Bengoshi Rengokai (Japan Federation of Bar Associations). Todo-shasuiheki-tou Fukushima Daiichi Genpatsu Osensusi Shori Taisaku no Mondaiten (Frozen Wall Water Barrier and Fukushima Daiichi Contaminated Water Issues). 2014. Available from: https://www.nichibenren.or.jp/library/ja/event/data/2014/event_141125_3_2.pdf

[18] The Committee for Reforming Tokyo Electric Power and Overcoming 1F Challenges. Toden Kaikaku Teigen (recommendations for TEPCO reform). 2016. Available from: http://www.meti.go.jp/committee/kenkyukai/energy_environment/touden_1f/pdf/161220_teigen.pdf

[19] Japan Center for Economic Research (JCER). Jiko Shorihiyo wa 50 cho~70 choen ninaru Osore (Total Costs of the Accident may go up to 50-70 trillion yen). 2017. Available from: https://www.jcer.or.jp/policy-proposals/20180824-13.html

[20] Tokyo Electric Power (TEPCO). Published at the Public Hearing by the Subcommittee on Treatment of Contaminated Water. 2018. Available from: http://www.meti.go.jp/earthquake/nuclear/osensuitaisaku/committtee/takakusyu/pdf/HPup3rd/5siryo.pdf

[21] Kino R. Torichiumu to Mizu to seifu wa yobukedo jissai niwa tano houshasei bussitsuga 1nende 65kai mo kijyun choka (Although the Government Calls Tritium Water, it Contains Other Radioactive Materials Beyond Regulatory Standards 65 Times in One Year). Yahoo! News. 2018. Available from: https://news.yahoo.co.jp/byline/kinoryuichi/20180827-00094631/

[22] Science Council of Japan. Regarding Final Disposal of High level Radioactive Waste. Answers to the Japan Atomic Energy Commission. 2012. Available from: http://www.scj.go.jp/ja/info/kohyo/pdf/kohyo-22-k159-1.pdf

[23] Japan Atomic Energy Commission (JAEC). Renewing Approaches to Geological Disposal of High-Level Radioactive Waste (HLW). 2012. Available from: http://www.aec.go.jp/jicst/NC/about/kettei/121218_e.pdf

[24] Ministry of Economy Trade and Industry (METI). Working Group on High-level Radioactive Waste, Interim Report (in Japanese). 2014. Available from: http://www.meti.go.jp/committee/sougouenergy/denryoku_gas/genshiryoku/houshasei_haikibutsu_wg/report_001.pdf

[25] Ministry of Economy Trade and Industry (METI). Tokutei Houshasei Haikibutsu ni kansuru Kihon Hoshin (Basic Policy on Final Disposal of Specified Radioactive Waste) (in Japanese). 2015. Available from: http://www.meti.go.jp/press/2015/05/20150522003/20150522003-1.pdf

[26] Shimbun NK. Kaku no Gomi Setsumeikai, Aratani 79nin yobikake hannmei (It is Now Revealed

that 79 More People were Paid to Attend the Nuclear Waste Public Meeting). 2017. Available from: https://www.nikkei.com/article/DGXMZO25163420X21C17A2CR8000/

[27] Science Council of Japan. Policy proposal for final disposal of high-level radioactive waste—Temporal storage for gaining national consensus. 2015. Available from: http://www.scj.go.jp/ja/info/kohyo/pdf/kohyo-23-t212-1.pdf

[28] Office of Atomic Energy Policy, Cabinet Office. The Status Report of Plutonium Management in Japan 2017. 2018. Available from: http://www.aec.go.jp/jicst/NC/about/kettei/180731_e.pdf

[29] Takubo M, von Hippel F. Ending Reprocessing in Japan; An Alternative Approach to Managing Japan's Spent Nuclear Fuel and Separated Plutonium. International Panel on Fissile Material (IPFM) Report. 2013. Available from: http://fissilematerials.org/library/rr12.pdf

[30] Press K. U.S. would back a rethink of Japan's plutonium recycling program: White House. The Japan Times. 2016. Available from: http://www.japantimes.co.jp/news/2016/05/21/national/politics-diplomacy/u-s-back-rethink-japans-plutonium-recycling-program-white-house/#.V1PF1PRAqD_.twitter

[31] Sakolski H. Can East Asia avoid a nuclear explosive materials arms race?. The Bulletin of Atomic Scientists. 2016. Available from: http://thebulletin.org/can-east-asia-avoid-nuclear-explosive-materials-arms-race9295

[32] Japan Atomic Energy Commission. The Basic Principles on Japan's Utilization of Plutonium. 2018. Available from: http://www.aec.go.jp/jicst/NC/iinkai/teirei/3-3set.pdf

[33] PuPo. 2017 Statement, Tokyo. 2017. Available from: http://www.cnic.jp/wp/wp-content/uploads/2017/02/PuPo-StatementFeb24FINAL.pdf

[34] Kuperman A. Japan's misguided plutonium policy. Arms Control Today. 2018. Available from: https://www.armscontrol.org/act/2018-10/features/japan%E2%80%99s-misguided-plutonium-policy

[35] New Diplomacy Initiative, Japan. Purutoniumu Sakugen ni Muketa Jitsugensei No Aru Sentakushiwo—Nihon No Purutoniumu Seisaku no Hensen (Feasible options are needed to reduce plutonium stockpile—Transition of Plutonium Policy in Japan). ND Policy Brief. Vol. 3. 2018. Available from: http://www.nd-initiative.org/research/5638/

[36] The National Diet of Japan. The Official Report of the Fukushima Nuclear Accident Independent Investigation Commission; 2012. https://www.nirs.org/wp-content/uploads/fukushima/naiic_report.pdf

Section 4

Implementation of Other Energy Technologies and Policies

Chapter 7

Acoustic Filters for Sensors and Transducers: Energy Policy Instrument for Monitoring and Evaluating Holy Places and Their Habitants

Himanshu Dehra

Abstract

The aim of the study is to present a brief overview of energy policy instrument for monitoring and evaluating holy places and their habitants with the aid of acoustic filters for sensors and transducers. A monitoring protocol for policy instrument is presented for noise protection and security from power systems. Methods of information and data collection are briefly elaborated. The power systems are classified as per source signals of solar power, electric power, light power, sound power, heat power, fluid power and fire power. The acoustic filters as per source of noise signals from power systems are defined. The filters are differentiated as per source signal of unwanted frequencies from solar power, electric power, light power, sound power, heat power, fluid power and fire power. Some examples of acoustic filters are mentioned as per source of noise signal. A slide rule for noise measurement is illustrated along with its noise grades and flag colors under limiting conditions. Some noise filtering results from various power systems of an outdoor duct are also tabulated. An overview of noise systems integration with command and control center is described. A brief discussion on management of holy places and their habitants through monitoring and evaluation is also mentioned.

Keywords: source, security, power system, signal, acoustic filter, sink, resonance, holy place, monitoring

1. Introduction

With increasing demands of worshiping, the world's holy places are congesting at an alarming rate. Many reasons are attributed to this crowding, some of which are given below:

- Growing human and worshipers' population;
- Increased purchasing power, high standard of living, and ease of travel caused sprawl at holy places;

- Increase in spiritual life style and thoughts with diversion from main stream of life because of increase in unemployment and dissatisfaction rates;
- Increase in awareness and beliefs about various faiths and religions.

1.1 Pressures on holy places

The growing pressures on holy places are leading to degradation of land and water bodies besides causing noise due to unwanted physical agents (heat, fluid, electricity, light, sound and fire) at these places [1]. The sprawl and congestion at Holy places is narrowing the access to the human resource base, especially for rural poor, who are directly dependent on these places of worships for their day to day existence. In addition, it has resulted in a serious local shortage of material resources, which is affecting the global economy and people in all walks of life.

'Noise' is defined as a sensation of unwanted intensity of a wave, is a perception of pollutant and a type of environmental stressor [2]. An environmental stressor of noise can have detrimental effects on various aspects of health. It is important to filter out unwanted intensity of wave from power systems (such as heat, fluid, electricity, light, sound, fire and sun) with use of acoustic filters for sensors and transducers after proper signal conditioning. This chapter contains basic introduction on monitoring and its protocol for the policy instrument on noise protection and security from power systems at holy places. Lot of noise and discomfort levels has been observed due to crowding and unwanted physical agents at holy places. The effects of unwanted physical agents from various power systems at holy places need to be thoroughly investigated.

The power systems are classified as per source signals of solar power, electric power, light power, sound power, heat power, fluid power and fire power [1]. The acoustic filters as per source of noise signals are defined [1–12]. The filters are differentiated as per source signal of unwanted frequencies from solar power, electric power, light power, sound power, heat power, fluid power and fire power. Some examples of acoustic filters for sensors and transducers with their energy balance for a human brain along with human comfort and health are exemplified [1, 2]. A slide rule for noise measurement is illustrated along with noise grades and flag colors under limiting conditions [1, 2]. Detail discussions on dynamics of holy places are also presented later in the chapter.

1.2 Literature review

There are various aspects of studying power systems. Numerous studies are conducted on power systems from energy and economic point of view. Taner and Demirci [13] presented energy and economic analysis of the wind turbine plant's draft for the Aksaray city. A 1 MW of the wind turbine plant was calculated for energy and economic analysis. Taner [14] conducted scenario analysis for a wind power plant in the Cappadocia region. The region was selected due to its high wind potential. This study determined that the construction of wind power plant can be suitable for the Cappadocia region by using the escalation method of inflation. Topal et al. [15] studied the significance of a trigeneration (TG) system. In this theoretical study, a trigeneration system converts a single fuel source into three useful energy products (i.e. power, heating and cooling), and focuses on the simulation with direct co-combustion of poultry wastes. Taner et al. [16] presented a case study of energy management in a sugar factory in Turkey. The study has analyzed energy consumption, the quantity of material production, and figure out a suitable energy efficiency measures for the sugar factory. Topal et al. [17] performed thermodynamic analysis on Çan Circulating Fluidized Bed Power Plant (CFBPP) co-fired with olive pits. Taner and Sivrioglu [18] conducted energy and exergy analysis of a model sugar factory in Turkey. The study determines the best energy and exergy efficiency with mass and energy balances as per design parameters for a sugar factory. Taner [19] studied the optimization processes of energy efficiency for a drying plant. The objective of study was to find the optimum energy and exergy efficiencies for the drying plant (production of bulgur). Taner [20] studied the performance of a proton exchange membrane (PEM) fuel cell with variation of its pressure and voltage parameters. The objective of the study was to improve the performance, efficiency and development of modeling and simulations of PEM fuel cells with aid of experimental optimization. Taner and Sivrioglu [21] developed a general model (sugar production processes) based on data provided by a real plant through an exergy analysis. The study explored the improvement of performance indicators of a turbine power plant through thermoeconomic analysis.

Some studies are also conducted on monitoring of pilgrims of holy places. Suryavanshi and Pandita [22] developed Wireless Sensor Network (WSN) based parameters for each pilgrim, who is equipped with a mobile unit which consists of micro-controller, GPS, GSM module, LCD, heartbeat sensor, temperature sensor, keypad and battery. Server unit initiate and transmit the query to mobile unit. On receiving the query by Mobile unit, it transmits its UID, latitude, longitude and a time stamp as a reply of received query to the server. Rajwade and Gawali [23] presented a real-time pilgrim tracking and health monitoring system, which was designed and implemented using Arduino in order to help the authority solve problem of pilgrim tracking and health monitoring system. A wearable unit was provided to each pilgrim for sensing the location and vital health parameters of that person. The authority in the control room was connected to the wearable unit using global system for mobile communication. The significance of this system is benefits to both pilgrims as well as to the authority.

Studies are also conducted on acoustic and other comfort parameters at religious places and mosques. Adnan et al. [24] presented a study to assess the acoustic quality level of three public mosques in Batu Pahat. They presented that good acoustic quality is necessary for appreciation in prayers. Karaman and Guzel [25] investigated the objective parameters of sound for the main prayer hall of the Bedirye Tiryaki Mencik Mosque in Manisa (Turkey). Prawirasasra and Mubarok [26] studied Syamsul Ulum Mosque (MSU) located at Telkom University, Indonesia for its actual acoustic condition and acoustical design. Main hall was considered as primary venue and is taken as analysis area. Measurements of the mosque covered only speech-related objective parameters; reverberation time (RT), Definition (D50), Sound Strength (G) and Noise Criteria (NC). Gul and Calıskan [27] discussed the design issues of a contemporary mosque, namely, Dogramacızade Ali Pasa Mosque in Ankara, Turkey. Architectural design parameters are evaluated supported with acoustical parameters with aid of computer simulation. Sezer and Kaymaz [28] studied users' perception of indoor environmental conditions in historical mosques in Turkey. The study focused on thermal, visual and acoustical comfort. For this purpose, a user's satisfaction survey was conducted to eight historical mosques' users in Bursa.

Few relevant papers on wind energy conversion and their annoying effects are briefed here. The annoying effects of wind energy conversion were investigated by Pohl et al. [29]. The study combined the methodology of stress psychology with noise measurement with an integrated approach and residents of a wind farm in Lower Saxony were interviewed on two occasions (2012, 2014) and given the opportunity to use audio equipment to record annoying noise. In another study, Krug and Lewke [30] presented a general overview on electromagnetic interference (EMI) with respect to mega-watt wind turbines. Possibilities of measuring all types of electromagnetic interference were explained with emphasis on a GSM transmitter mounted on a mega-watt wind turbine. Karpat and Karpat [31] reviewed and discussed electromagnetic compatibility (EMC) for a wind turbine.

1.3 Possible solutions

The need of the hour is to conserve these holy places and their habitants. This however requires long term planning and judicious management, developed on the basis of sound scientific knowledge on the status and dynamics of the different holy places and their habitants along with their interaction with the environment and their physical agents. Such information is few and far apart, resulting in a poor understanding of the noise systems at these places.

It is essential therefore to generate a global data base on the present condition of the different noise system parameters at these places. Developing such an information bank, is not easy task, for at following reasons: (i) the existing diversity in noise systems at these places, because of wide variations in climate, topography, land use patterns, noise types, life forms and human societies makes this task immense; and (ii) this diversity in noise systems and human societies, have resulted in very distinct resource use patterns that are area specific.

The data when generated could be used for local specific planning of holy sites, participatory management and appropriate conservation strategies.

1.4 Micro-planning

Micro-planning also referred to as local or decentralized planning is probably necessary for efficient use, management and conservation of holy places [32]. The best source of such information would be the local communities who regularly use these holy places for their basic survival needs, though very little has been learnt from them. Local specific data is therefore scarce, and collecting them is not easy job.

One method of achieving this goal would be, to promote studies on monitoring noise system data parameters at these holy places. Involving the literate local communities, youth and non-governmental organizations, in the task of monitoring, could be one way of solving this problem. Local people with collaboration of experts monitoring their own local habitants as well as monitoring their data would be more effective.

1.5 Importance of monitoring

- Monitoring is a tool, that could be used for developing a data base for micro level planning;

- Monitoring is a process of inventory repeated at regular intervals of time, which can be used for building ongoing or continuous data base of noise systems parameters at holy places and their habitants;

- The first study on a given parameter may be used as the baseline data or information used for comparisons with the periodically monitored information;

- Monitoring gives an in depth understanding of the status and dynamics of the noise data resources in the ecosystem;

- It identifies the needs of the community;
- It helps in evaluating people's own actions;
- It promotes better resource planning both at the individual level and at the community level;
- It gives a continuous feedback during project implementation thus ensuring quality;
- It helps in evaluating real-time data base of noise systems;
- It provides an information base for future projects;
- It furnishes information for decision makers;
- Monitoring is therefore an essential aspect of noise systems resource planning and management.

1.6 Noise systems monitoring methods: an ecosystem approach

As stated by Odum (1983), the term ecosystem means 'systems of the environment'. Thus, the physical environment in a given area or unit, with all the living components there, together with the network of interactions among these people and with their physical environment constitutes an ecosystem [32].

1.6.1 Collection of essential information on the ecosystem

The first part in noise systems monitoring study is to define a geographical area of the holy place where the study is to be conducted. Once the study area is selected, some important background information about this region needs to be collected in order to plan and conduct a scientific study on noise systems monitoring. This information is mainly on two aspects of the chosen study area, namely the socio-economic features and acoustic filters use patterns.

Given below is a list of background information that may be collected from the ecosystem of holy places and their habitants:

- Historical and cultural information about the area (e.g. changes in soil quality, water quality and its availability, traditional spiritual practices etc.);
- Information on social, economic, educational, demographic (local and transit population), health and development activities;
- Maps of the land;
- Soil conditions;
- Facts on water resources, rainfall, solar and temperature pattern;
- Data on all the households in the noise ecosystem;
- Information on acoustic filters use pattern and their topography.

2. Monitoring protocol

The theory of 'Acoustic filters for sensors and transducers' as proposed by the author is used in designing energy policy instrument for monitoring and evaluation of holy places and their habitants [1]. The noise data monitoring protocol has to be structured with a systematic approach. Depending upon interaction with local authorities of the holy places, a specific region specific monitoring protocol can be established on a case to case basis.

A monitoring protocol and its questionnaire can be used for survey of noise ecosystem at holy places. These questionnaires are related to the monitoring and assessment of noise that has to be abated. These noise monitoring surveys are conducted for variety of reasons. These can be: (i) evaluation of current noise levels at holy places; (ii) assess the noise exposure of habitants in their dwellings; (iii) identify sources of noise; (iv) establish a base line data for noise; (v) establish community response through measurement and verification of noise data; (vi) establish laws and legislation for setting up permissible noise levels; and (vii) develop and validate noise models for simulation.

In the monitoring survey, for each parameter the following are explained: (i) the aim of monitoring; (ii) importance of monitoring; (iii) sampling techniques; (iv) the procedure to be followed; and (v) recording and analysis of information. Points that can be considered while taking up a monitoring program: (i) visits to holy places should be structured and informed well in advance; (ii) appropriate modifications can be adopted for field methods depending on local conditions; (iii) developing a good relationship with the local people and organizations is necessary for field monitoring; and (iv) certain rules and precautions should be adopted during the field work depending upon faith and religion.

2.1 Methods of information collection

The first step in noise monitoring program is to collect scientifically sound information or data which can be used for further analysis and interpretation. This can be achieved by appropriate procedures to the noise parameter that is to be investigated. Sampling methods simplify the process of collecting scientifically accurate information. Such data can be used for further analysis to reveal reliable patterns and features of the parameters of the noise monitoring study.

2.1.1 Data collection

This is the first step for a noise monitoring investigation. Utmost care should be taken while collecting the data. A description of data collection methods is briefed here. There are two distinct methods of data collection. Primary and Secondary; Primary data collection involves data that is directly collected during the process of investigation. Secondary data collection involves data that is collected from different sources (i.e. data that is already available).

Methods of primary data collection include: (i) tapping the local knowledge; and (ii) direct measurements. In tapping the local knowledge, the members of the local community are an excellent source of information. They can provide valuable information on the local data. Two methods may be employed to collect information from the local source: (i) formal interviews; and (ii) informal interviews and participant observation. In both the above methods the investigator directly contacts the local inhabitants from whom the information has to be collected. Formal interviews are conducted when: (i) the objectives of the study are clearly defined prior to the interview; and (ii) the contents of the interview are distinctly listed. A structured questionnaire is generally used for this purpose.

2.1.2 Questionnaire

A questionnaire consists of a list of questions related to the noise monitoring investigation [33]. This is prepared by the investigator who collects the information in the space provided in the questionnaire.

Preparation of questionnaire requires a great deal of understanding and thought about the noise system and its affected ecosystem. Some general principles which may assist in drafting the questionnaire may consist of the following parameters:

- The number of questions should be kept to the minimum;
- The questions should be relevant to the objectives of the noise monitoring program;
- The questions should be short and in simple words. They should be unambiguous and easily understood;
- Questions should be arranged in a logical sequence such that, those pertaining to the background of the respondent (i.e. person who is being interviewed) should precede questions on the main information. The respondents could express their views toward the end of the questionnaire;
- As much as possible, the questions should be framed in such a way so as to extract brief, clear answers like 'yes' or 'no';

It is desirable to pre-test the questionnaire (i.e. try it once in the field) in order to check its effectiveness and to eliminate any drawbacks.

Informal interviews and careful observation of the subject often gives better information, as this method, does not have the obvious limitations of the formal approach. Here, the subject without being self-conscious may offer better information. In informal interviews, the number of questions should be limited and relevant to the objective so that the interviewer is able to recall the information later. The interviewer should document the information and observations as soon as possible after the informal interview.

In the direct measurements, the investigator directly measures to find out thc required information. Direct measurements can give better information on the various parameters that will be collected and analyzed. Sampling is an important tool which helps in better understanding the quality and quantity of an entire noise ecosystem of holy place and its habitants. When the study area is very large, an extensive study demands enormous amounts of money and human resources. A portion, or sub-set of the entire population referred to as a sample, is therefore chosen for a detailed assessment. Such a careful selection of sample is considered to be as good as examining the entire population. Sample size may be selected depending on: (i) degree of accuracy desired; (ii) time availability; (iii) available financial and other resources; and (iv) available manpower.

2.1.3 Sampling methods

There are many sampling methods for different kinds of ecological studies. In this manual simple random sampling and stratified random sampling are described because they are widely used. These methods result in more reliable representative distribution of samples.

The simple random sampling is used for a homogeneous population. In this technique sample selection is done randomly so that each and every section of the population has the same chance of being included in the sample. This process results in less chance of bias. There are two methods: (a) Lottery method: This is followed to ensure the randomness. In order to use this method for selecting the samples, the names of all the items of the entire population are individually written on paper slips. The slips are folded and scrambled. The numbers are selected using the lottery method. This process is difficult to implement when the population is large. In small population, as the paper slips are taken out, the number of paper slips reduces in the lottery box. Therefore the chances of each paper slip being picked up increases. (b) Random table: To avoid the problems involved in the lottery method the table of random numbers is used. The random table has been tested for its randomness which is well established. Usually the random table gives the figures in four digits. In random sampling the sample size should be large.

Stratified sampling is done if the population is heterogeneous or is made of distinct groups. The population is first classified or divided into the different groups. For example, if a human population study is done in a village the population can be divided into sub groups based on the type of acoustic filters in different households. Each of these groups is distinct and forms a division. The households in a noise ecosystem can be classified according to their socio-economic status (and type of acoustic filter being one of the determining criteria). The stratified random sampling method is considered as the most satisfactory and efficient method as it gives more representative samples. It should be noted however that, great care should be taken while dividing the population into different groups.

Data collection is followed by presentation, analysis and interpretation. After the data collection, it is necessary to be aware of methods of organizing data and performing basic statistical calculations even before one begins the study. Organization involves classifying and tabulating the data collected which is then analyzed and presented in an orderly form.

Methods of secondary data collection involve the information which is already available from different sources and should be collected prior to the field investigation and measurements. These can be: (i) recorded information, which are published data from governmental and non-governmental agencies, scientific institutions and historical records; and (ii) group discussions with the local community, which involve informal group discussions with members of the local community can yield valuable information. This helps in identifying some of the salient features of the ecosystem or community to be studied, which in turn helps in deciding on the noise system parameters that are important in that ecosystem. This also helps in building good rapport with the local community which is essential to collect good information. Discussions can also be held with a few key informants. Maps are essential tools in the monitoring exercise. They give quantitative information on a geographical or spatial scale. Maps are simple, effective and can therefore be easily understood. One can visualize vast spatial information at a glance. Maps tell us exactly where the selected study area is, and in addition, gives details on the physical features of the holy place. This saves considerable amount of time in the field. Remote sensing is restricted to methods which use electromagnetic energy, to collect information on the different geographical features on the earth's surface. Based on the physical and chemical properties (tone, texture, shape and location), the different objects on the surface of earth, reflect, re-radiate or emit varying amounts of electromagnetic energy in different wave lengths. The measurements of the reflected, re-radiated or emitted electromagnetic radiation, forms the basis for understanding the characteristic features on the earth. These typical responses are used to distinguish the objects from one another.

2.2 Data interpretation and report making

Interpretation is making conclusions based on the analyzed data. This is the most important part of the investigation. The data is interpreted based on the trends, patterns, principles of noise ecosystem and its concepts. The information thus analyzed and interpreted requires to be communicated to different groups of the community and various stakeholders like, decision makers and planners, researchers, students and general population. Report making is one method of communicating the findings to these target groups. The language and method used in preparing the report should vary depending on the group for whom it is aimed.

2.2.1 Data interpretation

Interpretation helps to take decisions and plan developmental work. The whole task of investigation fails if the conclusions drawn are not correct. A wrong or incomplete interpretation may mislead the decision making process. While interpretation of data, other associated and related factors should be considered.

In interpretation of data, following points should be considered:

- Bias or preconception must be avoided while interpreting data. Conscious or unconscious bias on the part of the investigator leads to false interpretations;
- While making comparisons there should be consistency in defining the noise monitoring parameters under study;
- General conclusions should not be made based on inadequate data. Conclusions driven based on micro-level data of noise ecosystem should not be generalized or extrapolated at the micro-level;
- While interpreting the data, other relevant variables should be considered. This is applicable specially to noise ecosystems as the interactions between the different factors are too many;
- Smaller differences should not be neglected as these may lead to important conclusions;
- Devising of any hypothesis should be supported with sufficient data.

2.2.2 Report making

Report making can be done in different ways. Three forms of report are: (i) a scientific reporting for researchers, students, teachers and other stakeholders who are involved in similar investigations; (ii) reporting for planners and decision makers and other governance officials; and (iii) reporting for literate local communities.

Scientific reporting gives a detailed account of the investigation and includes the methodology, data and a complete view of holy places and their dynamics. It should also analyze the findings and give possible reasons for them. Such report helps in comparative analysis of various noise ecosystems. A detailed account of the material and methods used for investigation should be provided. It is important to clearly describe the procedures followed in the investigation. Any noise ecosystem study should have a description of the holy site. A description of the holy site should include its historical, social and cultural background, weather, soil conditions, demographic factors and acoustic filters use pattern. Tables, diagrams, graphs and photographs should be used to support the description. This is for easy understanding and interpretation of the results of the investigation. The holy site description is followed by description of results, discussions, future planning, summary and references.

Reporting for planners and decision makers and other governance officials do not have much interest in detailed and technical scientific reports. This group is normally interested in the planning. Time may also be constraint for this group, therefore a report targeted for this group should be brief and clear and may contain brief and easy to understand sections of site description, status of noise ecosystem, conclusions and future planning. Future planning section is of major importance to the target group. The proposed plan for holy place and its noise ecosystem must be explained from the ecological, economic, social and cultural points of view with adequate figures to support it. Both the benefits and drawbacks of the plan should be discussed.

Reporting for the literate local community should be simple, brief and clear. Too many technical details should be avoided. The report should revolve around the community's interest. In the introductory part the importance and objectives of the study with reference to the community should be highlighted. Data which is relevant to the welfare of the community should be presented as simple as possible. Important conclusions drawn from the study should be emphasized. The proposed plan and the projected benefits as well as the possible drawbacks associated with it in terms of ecological, economic, social, and cultural considerations should be explained with brief discussions. The role of community members in the proposed plan should be mentioned. Any new technological information to be presented should be simplified with clarity. It is a good idea to provide the brief know how of the technology, with name of the provider and contact person.

3. Theory of acoustic filters for sensors and transducers

The displacement for any charged particle is defined by change of its position. A displacement has length and direction. The physical quantities that have features like displacements are called vectors. Vectors have both magnitude and direction and combine as per rules of addition. The physical quantities that are defined by number and unit and that only have magnitude are called scalars. The behavior of gases over wide range of temperatures is predicted through kinetic theory model by average kinetic energy of translation.

In collisions with the source of an energy such as due to firing in air at the kinetic velocity of a bullet of a gun, the rotational and vibrational modes of motion are excited, which contribute to the internal energy of the air for propagation of sound waves. The total energy consists of kinetic energy of translation and kinetic energy of vibration of atoms in a molecule and potential energy of vibration of the atoms in a molecule. The magnetic energy also contributes to the total energy, however the available energy depends only on the temperature and has distribution of equal parts to each of the independent ways in which the molecules are able to absorb energy. The theorem (mention here, with no proof) is called equipartition of energy was deduced by James Clerk Maxwell. Each such independent way of absorbing energy is termed as degree of freedom for a molecule of gas.

The acoustic filters are defined based on the model of kinetic theory of gases for filtering unwanted frequencies of oscillations from a power system. It is a network with selective transmission for currents from a power system of varying frequency. A new theory for noise protection and security from power systems is presented. An acoustic filter is used to filter unwanted frequencies of oscillations from a power system. It is a network with selective transmission for currents from a power system of varying frequency. The noise protection and security is a crucial operation for obtaining a desired output from a power system.

The unwanted frequencies generated from a power system are removed by using an operational amplifier with different combination of filter arrangements. The filters are differentiated as per source signal of unwanted frequencies from solar power, electric power, light power, sound power, heat power, fluid power and fire power. The acoustic filter is an electrical analog circuit of various combinations of RC feedback circuit with an operational amplifier [1–7].

3.1 Operational amplifier

An operational amplifier is an integrated circuit that consists of several bipolar transistors, resistors, diodes, and capacitors, interconnected so that amplification can be achieved over a wide range of frequencies. The open loop configuration of an operational amplifier has the highest possible gain when running wide open. In the closed loop configuration, it is easy to control the gain due to negative feedback. This feedback is obtained by connecting the output to the inverting input through a potentiometer. The negative feedback is useful for volume control of a highly versatile amplifier. The gain in closed loop configuration is directly proportional to the feedback loop resistance.

3.2 Acoustic filters

The action of filtering the frequency from a power system is based on the variation in the reactance of an inductance or a capacitance with the frequency. The band of frequencies that can be removed from a power system can be at the low frequency end of frequency spectrum, at the high frequency end, at both ends, or in the middle of the spectrum. The filters to perform each of these operations are known respectively as low-pass filters, high-pass filters, band-pass filters and band-stop filters. There are many configurations of design of filters. The filters are divided into passive and active configurations. The passive filters are less effective simple circuits constructed with resistors, capacitors, and inductors. The active filters are useful in providing an effective filtering action than passive filters. The active filters require a source of operating power.

3.3 Acoustic filter systems

The criteria for definitions of filters for noise filtering is based on areas of energy stored in a wave due to noise interference, speed of wave and difference of power between two intensities of wave [6]. The filtered noise signals are considered from systems of solar power, electric power, light power, sound power, heat power, fluid power and fire power. The acoustic filters as per sources of noise are defined [12].

3.3.1 Filter for noise of sol

This filter is used to filter noise due to power intensities difference between two solar power systems. Example: window curtain, window blind, wall and sunglasses.

3.3.2 Filter for noise of therm

This filter is used to filter noise due to power intensities difference between two heat power systems. Example: house, insulation, clothing and furnace.

3.3.3 Filter for noise of photons

This filter is used to filter noise due to power intensities difference between two lighting systems. Example: 3-D vision of any object, cell-phone, electric bulb, television, computer and LCD screen laptop.

3.3.4 Filter for noise of electrons

This filter is used to filter noise due to power intensities difference between two electrical power systems. Example: AM/FM radio clock with ear phones, telephone instrument with ear phones, cell-phone with ear phones and CD audio player with ear phones.

3.3.5 Filter for noise of scattering

This filter is used to filter noise due to power intensities difference between two fluid power systems. Example: electric fan, pump, motor vehicle, river stream and tap water.

3.3.6 Filter for noise of scattering and lightning

This filter is used to filter noise due to power intensities difference between two fire power systems. Example: lighter, matchstick, gas stove, locomotive engine and thunder-bolt.

3.3.7 Filter for noise of elasticity

This filter is used to filter noise due to power intensities difference between two sound power systems. Example: your vocal chords, organ pipe, thunder-bolt and drum beats.

4. Sensors and transducers: energy balance for a human brain

Your body has feedback systems that regulate the internal environment of your body. The feedback systems make use of storage depots and numerous feedback loops. The monitoring of plasma calcium is a good example of negative feedback. The bones constitute large storage depots for calcium, for the plasma to withdraw these storage supplies in times of need. Our body's homeostatic regulatory systems are represented by feedback loops. The feedback is considered negative, when it is compensating or negates any change. The negative feedback is essential to stabilize a system. The gastrointestinal tract, the lungs, the kidneys, and skin of your body make exchange of materials and energy between the internal and the external environments. A steady state is achieved by regulatory mechanisms involving the balance between the inflow and outflow of the internal environment that stabilizes the composition of the internal environment. The tendency to regulate the internal environment so that it is maintained in a steady state is called homeostasis.

The keeping of face beard (facial hair) and wearing of a knitted head cloth (*patka*) and a turban (*pag*) on your body has a logical and a scientific significance. The daily self-making folds of hair knots and making round folds of turban over the head of your body with colorful cotton cloths has following historical, medical benefits: (i) it indicate, protects and concentrate the disciplinary physical and mental strength of a person; (ii) it gives hair tonic to the growth of hairs on your body due to solar energy;

(iii) the whole system acts as an acoustic filter and provides immunity to your body; and (iv) the folded *Patka* with style, folded design of hair knots on top of your head is your identity in time domain, the face beard on your body is a measuring ration and a sign of man, the turban with style, color, design is your identity in space domain.

The energy generated by metabolism rate of your body varies considerably with the activity of your body. A unit to express the metabolic rate per unit of area of your body is termed as met (1 met = 58.2 W m^{-2}), defined as the metabolic rate for your body while seated quite (called sedentary). The variable which affects the comfort of your body is the type and amount of clothing that you are wearing. The insulation of clothing is defined as a single equivalent uniform layer over your whole body. The insulation value for clothing of your body is expressed in terms of clo units (1 clo = 0.155 m^2-C W^{-1}). A heavy business suit with accessories has insulation value of 1 clo, whereas a pair of shorts has 0.05 clo.

5. Results: a slide rule for noise measurement

Table 1 has summarized units of noise and their limiting conditions [8–12]. **Table 1** has also notated grades and flag colors under limiting conditions.

Figure 1 has presented a double-sided hexagonal slide rule with seven edges for noise measurement representing seven sources of noise. Reference value used for I_2 is −1 W m^{-2} on positive scale of noise and 1 W m^{-2} on negative scale of noise. Positive scale of noise has 10 positive units and one negative unit. Whereas,

Grades	Noise Grades and Flag Colors under Limiting Conditions		
	Noise of Sol	*Noise of Scattering*	*Noise of Elasticity*
$G_2{}^a = \pm U$	Sol	Sip	Bel
$G_1 = G_2 = U$	No Positive Solar Energy	No Positive Fluid Energy	No Positive Sound Energy
Base Color for $G_1 = G_2$			
$G_1 = U{+}{\to}0$ Wm^{-2}	Decreasing Solar Energy	Decreasing Fluid Energy	Decreasing Sound Energy
Base Color for G_2			
$G_1 = +$ ve	Increasing Solar Energy	Increasing Fluid Energy	Increasing Sound Energy
Base Color for G_2			
$G_1 = -U$ Wm^{-2}	Negative Solar Energy	Negative Fluid Energy	Negative Sound Energy
	Darkness	Low Pressure	Inaudible range
Base Color for G_2			
$G_1 = -$ve	Darkness increasing, distance from point source of light increasing	Low pressure increasing, vacuum approaching	Inaudible range increasing, vacuum approaching
Base Color for G_2			
$G_1 = -U{+}{\to}0$ Wm^{-2}	Negative Solar Energy	Negative Fluid Energy	Negative Sound Energy
	Decreasing Darkness	Decreasing Low Pressure	Decreasing inaudible range
Base Color for G_2			

[a]*Reference value of $G_2 = \pm U$ signifies the limiting condition with areas of noise interference approaching to zero.*

Table 1.
Noise grades and flag colors under limiting conditions.

negative scale of noise has 1 positive unit and 10 negative units. Each unit of sol, sip and bel is divided into 11 parts, 1 part is 1/11th unit of noise. The base of logarithm used in noise measurement equations is 11.

The results of noise filtering using various noise measurement equations for an outdoor duct exposed to solar radiation are tabulated in **Tables 2–5** [2].

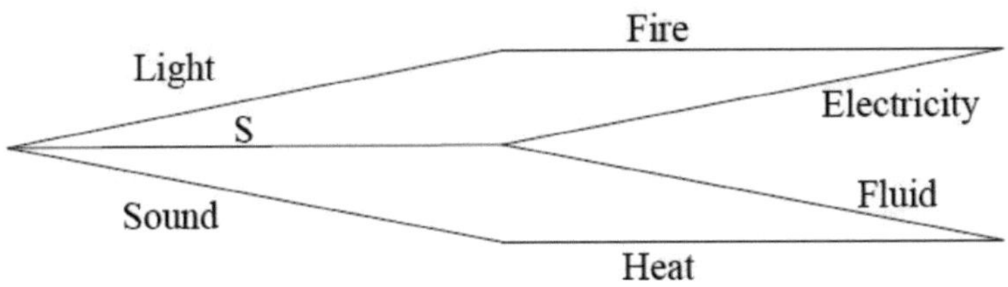

Figure 1.
A double sided hexagonal scales of noise with seven edges (S denotes sun).

Solar irradiation (W m^{-2})	Air temperature difference (ΔT) °C	Noise of sol oS (oncisol)
450	15.50	28
550	18.90	28.93
650	22.40	29.7
750	25.90	30.36
850	29.40	30.91

Table 2.
Temperature difference and noise of sol with solar irradiation (air velocity: 0.75 m s^{-1}).

Air velocity (m s^{-1})	Fluid power (W m^{-2})	Air temperature difference (ΔT) °C	Noise of scattering oS (oncisip)
1.35	47.62	15.28	17.72
1.05	37.0	18.22	16.50
0.75	26.45	22.40	15.02
0.45	15.87	28.15	12.65
0.15	05.29	29.80	07.64

Table 3.
Temperature difference and noise of scattering with air velocity (S = 650 W m^{-2}).

(ΔT) °C	Mass flow rate (Kg s^{-1})	Thermal power (W m^{-2})	Noise of therm oS (oncisol)	(ΔT) °C	Mass flow rate (Kg s^{-1})	Thermal power (W m^{-2})	Noise of therm oS (oncisol)
15.50	0.01376	71.09	19.5602	15.28	0.0231	117.65	21.868
18.90	0.01275	80.325	20.119	18.22	0.0171	103.85	21.296
22.40	0.0120	89.6	20.614	22.40	0.0120	89.6	20.614
25.90	0.0115	99.2833	21.043	28.15	8.1×10^{-3}	76.0	19.866
29.40	0.0111	108.78	21.505	29.80	6.2×10^{-3}	61.59	18.898

Table 4.
Mass flow rate and noise of therm with (ΔT) °C.

Air velocity ($m\ s^{-1}$)	Fluid power ($W\ m^{-2}$)	Noise of scattering oS (oncisip)	Sound pressure ($N\ m^{-2}$)	Sound power intensity ($W\ m^{-2}$)	Noise of elasticity oB (oncibel)
1.35	47.62	17.72	557.5	752.7	30.36
1.05	37.0	16.50	433.65	455.33	28.05
0.75	26.45	15.02	309.75	232.31	24.97
0.45	15.87	12.65	185.85	83.63	20.24
0.15	05.29	07.64	61.94	09.29	10.12

Table 5.
Noise of elasticity with air particle velocity (Impedance Z_0 = 413 N s m^{-3} at 20°C).

6. Integration of real-time noise system parameters with command and control center

Noise monitoring data of holy places and their habitants can be collected in real-time domain with aid of computerized monitor and control distributed systems at master location. The system is called Supervisory Control and Data Acquisition (SCADA). The control may be automatic, or initiated by operator commands. The data acquisition is accomplished firstly by the remote terminal units (RTU's) scanning the field inputs connected to the programmable logic controller (PLC). This is usually done at the fast rate. The central host will scan the RTU's usually at a slower rate. The data is processed to detect alarm conditions, and if an alarm is present, it will be displayed on special alarm lists. Data can be of three main types. Analogue data (i.e. real numbers) will be trended on data analytics software (i.e. placed in graphs). Digital data (on/off) may have alarms attached to one state or the other. Pulse data (e.g. counting revolutions of a meter or counter) is normally accumulated or counted.

A typical SCADA system includes remote sensors, controllers, or alarms located at facilities of holy places, as well as a central processing system situated in an appropriate location. SCADA systems integrate data acquisition systems with data transmission systems and graphical software in order to provide a centrally located monitor and control system for numerous process inputs and outputs. SCADA systems are designed to collect information, transfer it back to a central computer and display the information to the operators, thereby allowing the operator to monitor and control the entire noise system parameters from a central location in real time.

6.1 Components of SCADA system

SCADA system is composed of the following:

- Central Monitoring Station;
- Remote Terminal Units (RTUs);
- Field Instrumentation;
- Communications Network

The Central Monitoring Station (CMS) refers to the location of the master or host computer. Several workstations may be configured on the CMS. It uses a

Man Machine Interface (MMI) program to monitor various types of data needed for the operation. The Remote Station is installed at the remote points in the facilities being monitored and controlled by the central host computer. This can be a Remote Terminal Unit (RTU) or a Programmable Logic Controller. Field instrumentation refers to the sensors and actuators that are directly interfaced to the remote locations in the holy facilities. They generate the analog and digital signals that will be monitored by the Remote Station. Signals are also conditioned to make sure they are compatible with the inputs/outputs of the RTU or PLC at the Remote Station. The Communications Network is the medium for transferring information from one location to another. This can be via telephone line, radio or cable.

7. Discussions

A power system is defined as a power station with network of light, sound, heat, fluid, electricity, fire and sun, and its consumers living within its natural ecosystem vicinity area. Irrespective of the type of station, energy as a rule, produced on a centralized basis, which means that individual power stations supply energy to a common power grid and therefore, are combined into integrated power systems which may cover large territory with a larger number of consumers. Consumers are called habitants of the ecosystem vicinity area in the holy place.

Management of habitants through use of acoustic filters at the holy places from the perspective of protection from unwanted physical agents of various power systems is a need of time and a crucial energy policy tool. Thus management becomes the function of getting things done effectively by others. It is not just 'doing' – but 'doing well'. Management primarily is a function of managing people or habitants first and then comes the materials, equipment and systems. If habitants work properly, systems perform well automatically. Management is principally a task of planning, coordinating, motivating and controlling the efforts and interest of others to achieve a specific objective. The functions of management in general are: (i) planning; (ii) organizing; (iii) directing; (iv) coordinating; (v) controlling; and (vi) decision making.

Planning can be done for holy places and forecasting anticipated growth of habitants. Planning is an activity of anticipating the future and discovering alternative courses of action. It involves in-out-lining what, how, where, when and by whom a particular job has to be done. It is against random action. Planning is the rational and orderly thinking about ways and means of achieving certain goals. It involves thought and decision-pertaining to a future course of action. If there is no proper planning—rashness, short-sightedness, random-working or haphazard setup in the performance of work.

Proper organization of holy places is required so as to cater the mechanism for all the necessary things required for their proper monitoring and evaluation. Organizing involves: (i) determination of activities; (ii) determining staff and their requirements, developing and planning qualified people in various roles and responsibilities; (iii) allocation of work; (iv) determination of authority and duty; and (v) delegation of power. Organizations calls for the matching of roles and responsibilities with individuals in such a way personal contentment and social satisfaction of people, is addition to achieving their well-being.

Knowing well that management is the art of getting work done through the people, management plans, organizers and staff. Directing involves energizing the organizational mechanism, activating it or putting it into action to carry out the management plan. Human resources have emotions, aspirations, sentiments, capacities of their own, etc. Direction of human resources is through leadership, guidance, supervision, communication and counseling. Human aspect should not be overlooked. Workers should be made to carry out their roles and responsibilities willingly, wholeheartedly and with good team spirit.

Coordinating is a process of achieving team spirit and unity of action among human resources at all levels. Even there are people of different origins, different psychologies and interests, and different capacities are engaged in holy places, and if there is disharmony, and inefficiency, and if the workers are poorly selected or improperly placed at holy places, their performance is greatly weakened. Coordination is necessary to achieve and maintain harmony and a sound working balance. Coordination is the integration, synchronization or orderly pattern of group activities. Coordination should not be confused with cooperation. Cooperation implies collective efforts put in by a group voluntarily in any work. It has no time, quantity, or direction element in its observations. Both coordination and cooperation are essential for effective management. The disintegrating forces which adversely affect coordination are: (i) diverse and specialized activities; (ii) empire building tendencies; (iii) personal rivalries and jealousies; and (iv) conflict of interest.

Controlling is the process of measuring the results obtained and measuring the deviation or error between what is realized and what is expected from a system or device. If there is deviation, suitable corrections have to be effected so that, realized result is in full or close agreement with the targets or expected/desired results. Control—ensures both qualitative and quantitative performance of work. Proper control ensures accuracy. Control also brings to light, any lapses in the management, hindering the satisfactory progress of work. Controlling at holy places involves: (i) setting up of standards or yardsticks for habitants; (ii) assessment of actual performed work; (iii) determination of deviation; and (iv) corrective action.

Decision making, basically is the process or means of selecting one alternative out of two or more available alternatives. At holy places, decision making covers all functions of management. Good management performs its functions with wise, conscious, effective and appropriate decision making. Success of decision making is with good management, through their workers by sound judgements and quick logical divisions. Decision making can be done effectively through: (i) statement of problem; (ii) collecting or finding alternative solutions; (iii) through full study and management experiments; and (iv) final judicious choice. Aids for making decisions consist taking wise and judicious and practical decisions, which are highly critical, complicated and also requires deep imagination. The techniques which have been developed for decision making are: (i) operations research; (ii) linear programming; and (iii) break-even analysis. Computer systems at holy places can be used to solve problem of decision making. This is because it involves numerous data. Decisions with regard to future course of action are important concerning—inventory control, working conditions, cost price volumes, investments, etc.

7.1 Need for committees

(i) to study complex problems of holy places. These problems are beyond the capacity of single specialists. These committees are called investigating and advisory committees; (ii) for achieving control and coordination, so that unity of action results. The committees to work for this action are the standing committees, being permanent in structure and action; and (iii) to train the new staff, regarding the problems, policies of the holy places. Standing committees called education committees or dissemination committees are appointed for this purpose.

7.2 Dynamics of holy places

Changes in the structure and operation of holy places and their habitants are necessary for the reason that with modern times, the management of holy places should move with times. It can be changed in several ways, to keep it in turn with the managerial performance so that high quality output is realized. Any holy place should be flexible enough to get adjusted to get adapted to ever changing practices in operation, from time to time. The structure should be such that conflicts, misunderstandings and all forms of friction, inefficiencies, indiscipline and other negative factors of holy places are avoided and a serene informal atmosphere is created in it. One of the important and necessary results of the dynamics of holy places is to achieve from the top most level to the bottom most grades so that following shortcomings are totally avoided: (i) delay in decision making; (ii) frequent and serious errors in decision; (iii) bottlenecks; (iv) inadequate communication; (v) lack of clear-cut-objectives; and (vi) frequent and serious clashes among different groups and so on. The presence of any of the above or all the above indicates poor organization of holy place. If such anomalies and other negative traits occur, the changes are absolutely necessary. But what is called 'earthquake approach' to make unnecessary drastic changes-should be guarded against. Because of significant growth of holy places due to increase of consumerism, modern economy, quite far reaching alternations may become absolutely necessary. The main purpose of changes should be to minimize the disturbing effects. Long range plan is more productive than the earthquake approach. In this long-run plan changes are put into effect over a period of years.

7.3 Management systems

The management system at holy places is conceived as a multitude of elements being integrated and disintegrated in a random fashion. Consequently, it is difficult to reveal regularity and to define the system structure at holy places. However, for the system to perform its main function, consistent with the objective for which it has been devised, it is immaterial what the specific complexes will be, i.e., which facilities of holy places will be integrated in them. This implies that there must exist such a system structure that is sufficiently stable and adequately defines the system on hand. Two holy places having the same objective will never be exactly identical and consequently will have distinct structures. The differences occur as a result of different traditions, individual features of personnel and managerial staff, regional differences, and many other intangibles. However, these too must be embodied into a common framework from which an objective description may evolve in the form of an abstract structure. The approach of representing the management system as a purposeful process can be used at holy places. The goal programming method in which purposefulness peculiar to management systems is represented as an ordered structure of a tree of goals. This isolation of goals into an independent structure corresponds to a stratified approach in system theory, i.e., the structure of the goal stratum is evaluated. The goal stratum represents the system but from one side. The structure of goals is of static nature and gives only an indication of what is to be achieved, saying nothing of how this can be done. The functional structure is the one to answer this question, i.e., structuring in the functional stratum gives a clue to solve problems of evaluation and improvement of system performance. And, last but not the least, one should not overlook the physical structure of the system at holy place, which describes the relation between the physical objects or elements of the management system.

7.4 Modeling of management systems at holy places

To summarize the discussions, a generalized discussion of modeling of management system at holy places is briefed here. The generalized modeling of holy places can be pursued with the use of entropy maximization principle [34]. The holy places are like a transportation terminal or hub, in which devotees are arrived by different modules: (i) maritime; (ii) railroad; and (iii) highway. There are also: (iv) storage depots of materials; and (v) environmental interconnections. This structure of five modules reflects the actual structure of the holy places. The interactions with these different components of holy places are called events. Events in turn may be viewed as elements of the functional structure of the holy place system. On the one hand, they are induced by other elements, and on the other, they generate new elements themselves. In a module, each event is associated with a set of integer-valuable variables which have physical meaning owing to the simulating nature of the model. At the same time, these variables constitute a mechanism of interaction of modules. A variable being written in a module implies an event for this module. Variables being read out in a module mean that the events which are established for this module by another module are recorded. This pattern of simulation modeling requires that the events to be modeled occur at definite time instants and be respectively synchronized. This is achieved by imposing control on the time of modeling. In this model each module is connected with a timer, operating as a synchronizing clock. Modules operate step-wise. At each step of module operation all the events established for it by other modules are evaluated and the event for which time is right is recorded. As the processing of events goes by, the timer changes the current time.

All the modules of holy place system describe the processes of arrival and departures of the transportation facilities, operation of servicing of habitants. The module of storage of materials deals with the processes of accumulation and storage of goods with all transportation facilities. Accordingly, it records the events associated with the arrival and departure of habitants. The module responsible for the impacts of the environment models the probabilistic and independent pattern of arrival and departure of vehicles (of habitants and materials). Operating interactively with the model implemented on a computer, the analyst can adjust the values of the key variables so as to achieve a satisfactory performance of the entire holy place. The maximum entropy principle is realized in that the distribution of arrival of vehicles is reduced to a random process, and the rates of service processes and the vehicular units are averaged. The degree of generalization may be established by the analyst depending on the interpretation of the events and noise systems being modeled. Of course management systems at holy places are not thermodynamic and their structures are stable away from a thermodynamic equilibrium. Borrowing from the non-equilibrium terminology, these systems may be categorized as dissipative structures.

8. Conclusion

The chapter has introduced the energy policy instrument for noise protection and security by monitoring and evaluation of holy places and their habitants. A theory for noise protection and security with use of acoustic filters is presented. The acoustic filters for filtering noise from power systems are defined. The power systems are classified as per source signals of solar power, electric power, light power, sound power, heat power, fluid power and fire power. Some advanced level configurations of acoustic filters for different power systems are described. Sensors and transducers for a human brain are illustrated. The example of turban as an acoustic filter is illustrated. **Table 1** has presented the noise units under limiting conditions along with noise grades and flag colors. **Figure 1** has illustrated sketch of a slide rule for noise measurement. A brief overview of integration of noise systems parameters with command and control center is also presented. Discussions on dynamics and modeling of holy places from management perspective are also presented.

Author details

Himanshu Dehra
Egis India Consulting Engineers Pvt Ltd., Gurugram, Haryana, India

*Address all correspondence to: anshu_dehra@hotmail.com

References

[1] Dehra H. Acoustic filters for sensors and transducers. In: International Conference on Applied Energy (ICAE 2018), Hong Kong, China on Aug 22-25, 2018. Energy Procedia, Elsevier. 8 p. Available form: http://www.applied-energy.org/icae2018/

[2] Dehra H. A paradigm of noise interference in a wave. In: Internoise-2018, 47th International Congress and Exposition on Noise Control Engineering, Chicago, Illinois, USA on Aug 26-29, 2018. INCE, 12 p. Available from: https://internoise2018.org/

[3] Dehra H. A unified theory for stresses and oscillations. In: Proc. CAA Conf. Montréal, Sep 2007, Canada, Canadian Acoustics. 2007. Vol. 35, No. 3. pp. 132-133

[4] Dehra H. Acoustic filters, chapter 5. In: Romano VA, Duval AS, editors. Ventilation: Types, Standards and Problems. New York, USA: Nova Publishers; 2012. pp. 135-154

[5] Dehra H. A theory of acoustics in solar energy. Natural Resources. 2013;**4**(1A):116-120

[6] Dehra H. Power transfer and inductance in a star connected 3-phase RC circuit amplifier. In: Proc. AIChE 2008 Spring Meeting, New Orleans, LA, USA, Apr 6-10, 2008, session 96a. 7 p

[7] Dehra H. A novel theory of psychoacoustics on noise sources, noise measurements and noise filters. In: INCE Proc. NoiseCon16 Conf., Providence, Rhode Island, USA, Jun 13-15, 2016. pp. 933-942

[8] Dehra H. A slide rule for noise measurement. In: 10th International Conference on Sustainable Energy Technologies (SET 2011), Istanbul, Turkey, Sep 4-7, 2011. 5 p

[9] Dehra H. On sources and measurement units of noise. In: Proc. International Conference on Innovation, Management and Industrial Engineering (IMIE 2016), Kurume, Fukuoka, Japan, Aug 5-7 2016. pp. 219-227. ISSN: 2412-0170

[10] Dehra H. A paradigm for characterization and checking of a human noise behavior. In: WASET Proceedings of 19th International Conference on Psychological and Brain Sciences, May 11-12, 2017, Montréal, Canada. pp. 658-666. PISSN: 2010-376X, EISSN: 2010-3778

[11] Dehra H. A guide for signal processing of sensors and transducers. In: Proc. AIChE 2009 Spring Meeting, Tampa, FL, USA, Apr 26-30, 2009, session 6b. 2009. 9 p

[12] Dehra H. Acoustic signal processing and noise characterization theory via energy conversion in a PV solar wall device with ventilation through a room. Advances in Science, Technology and Engineering Systems Journal. 2018;**3**(4):130-172. Special Issue on Multidisciplinary Sciences and Engineering. DOI: 10.25046/aj030414

[13] Taner T, Demirci OK. Energy and economic analysis of the wind turbine plant's draft for the Aksaray City. Applied Ecology and Environmental Sciences. 2014;**2**(3):82-85. DOI: 10.12691/aees-2-3-2

[14] Taner T. Economic analysis of a wind power plant: A case study for the Cappadocia region. Journal of Mechanical Science and Technology;**32**(3):1379-1389. DOI: 10.1007/s12206-018-0241-6

[15] Topal H, Taner T, Altıncı Y, Amirabedin E. Application of trigeneration with direct co-combustion of poultry waste and coal: A case study

in the poultry industry from Turkey. Thermal Science. 2017 (in press). DOI: 10.2298/TSCI170210137T

[16] Taner T, Sivrioglu M, Topal H, Dalkilic AS, Wongwises S. A model of energy management analysis, case study of a sugar factory in Turkey. Sadhana 43 – Academy Proceedings in Engineering Sciences. 2018:1-20 Article no. 42. DOI: 10.1007/s12046-018-0793-2

[17] Topal H, Taner T, Naqvi Syed AH, Altınsoy Y, Amirabedin E, Ozkaymak M. Exergy analysis of a circulating fluidized bed power plant co-firing with olive pits: A case study of power plant in Turkey. Energy. 2017;**140**:40-46. DOI: 10.1016/j.energy.2017.08.042

[18] Taner T, Sivrioglu M. Energy-exergy analysis and optimisation of a model sugar factory in Turkey. Energy. 2015;**93**(1):641-654. DOI: 10.1016/j.energy.2015.09.007

[19] Taner T. Optimisation processes of energy efficiency for a drying plant: A case of study for Turkey. Applied Thermal Engineering. 2015;**80**:247-260. DOI: 10.1016/j.applthermaleng.2015.01.076

[20] Taner T. Energy and exergy analyze of PEM fuel cell: A case study of modeling and simulations. Energy. 2018;**143**:284-294. DOI: 10.1016/j.energy.2017.10.102

[21] Taner T, Sivrioglu M. A techno-economic & cost analysis of a turbine power plant: A case study for sugar plant. Renewable and Sustainable Energy Reviews. 2017;**78**:722-730. DOI: 10.1016/j.rser.2017.04.104

[22] Suryawanshi S, Pandita S. Pilgrim tracking and health monitoring system using WSN. International Journal of Advanced Research in Computer and Communication Engineering. 2015;**4**(12):172-175. DOI: 10.17148/IJARCCE.2015.41238

[23] Rajwade KC, Gawali DH. Wearable sensors based pilgrim tracking and health monitoring system. In: IEEE 2016 International Conference on Computing Communication Control and automation (ICCUBEA), Aug 12-13, 2016, Pune, India. DOI: 10.1109/ICCUBEA.2016.7860129

[24] Adnan NA, Shahminan RNR, Ibrahim FK, Tami H, Yusuff MRM, Samsudin EM, et al. Acoustic quality levels of mosques in Batu Pahat. In: IOP Conference Series: Earth and Environmental Science. Vol. 140. 2018. p. 012009. DOI: 10.1088/1755-1315/140/1/012009

[25] Karaman ÖY, Güzel NO. Acoustical properties of contemporary mosques case study of "Bedirye Tiryaki Mencik Mosque", Manisa, YBL, Journal of Built Environment. 2017;**5**(1):14-30. DOI: 10.1515/jbe-2017-0002

[26] Prawirasasra M S and Mubarok S. Evaluation of acoustical comfort in mosque, International Conference on Aerospace, Mechanical and Mechatronic Engineering IOP Publishing IOP Conf. Series: Materials Science and Engineering. Vol. 211. 2017. 5 p. 012021. DOI: 10.1088/1757-899X/211/1/012021

[27] Gul ZS, Calıskan M. Impact of design decisions on acoustical comfort parameters: Case study of Dogramacızade Ali Pasa Mosque. Applied Acoustics. 2013;**74**: 834-844

[28] Sezer FS, Kaymaz E. The user's perception of indoor comfort conditions in historical mosques: The case of Bursa. Turkey, International Journal of Humanities and Social Science. 2016;**6**(9):43-54

[29] Pohl J, Gabriel J, Hübner G. Understanding stress effects of wind turbine noise—The integrated approach. Energy Policy. 2018;**112**:119-128

[30] Krug F, Lewke B. Electromagnetic interference on large wind turbines. Energies. 2009;**2**:1118-1129. DOI: 10.3390/en20401118

[31] Karpat E, Karpat F. Electromagnetic compatibility (EMC) in wind turbines, Proceedings of 68th The IIER International Conference, Barcelona, Spain, Apr 13, 2016. pp. 3-6. ISBN: 978-93-85973-97-0

[32] Ravindranath S, Premnath S. Biomass Studies—Field Methods for Monitoring Biomass. Oxford & IBH Publishing Co. Pvt. Ltd, New Delhi; 1997

[33] WHO. In: Goelzer B, Hansen CH, Sehrndt GA, editors. Occupational Exposure to Noise: Evaluation, Prevention and Control. Geneva: World Health Organization; 1995. pp. 25-27

[34] Dehra H. The entropy matrix generated exergy model for a photovoltaic heat exchanger under critical operating conditions. International Journal of Exergy. 2008;**5**(2):132-149. Inderscience, ISSN online: 1742-8300. DOI: 10.1504/IJEX.2008.016671